BARKLEY FUNCTIONAL IMPAIRMENT SCALE (BFIS)

AF866721

Barkley Functional Impairment Scale (BFIS)

Russell A. Barkley

THE GUILFORD PRESS
New York London

A Division of Guilford Publications, Inc.
72 Spring Street, New York, NY 10012
www.guilford.com

Printed in the United States of America

This book is printed on acid-free paper.

Last digit is print number: 9 8 7 6 5 4 3 2 1

The author has checked with sources believed to be reliable in his efforts to provide information that is complete and generally in accord with the standards of practice that are accepted at the time of publication. However, in view of the possibility of human error or changes in medical sciences, neither the author, nor the editor and publisher, nor any other party who has been involved in the preparation or publication of this work warrants that the information contained herein is in every respect accurate or complete, and they are not responsible for any errors or omissions or the results obtained from the use of such information. Readers are encouraged to confirm the information contained in this book with other sources.

Library of Congress Cataloging-in-Publication Data
Barkley, Russell A., 1949–
Barkley functional impairment scale (BFIS) / Russell A. Barkley.
p. ; cm.
Includes bibliographical references and index.
ISBN 978-1-60918-219-9 (pbk.: alk. paper)
1. Psychiatric rating scales. 2. Life skills—Testing. I. Title.
[DNLM: 1. Activities of Daily Living. 2. Psychiatric Status Rating Scales. 3. Data Interpretation, Statistical. 4. Mental Disorders. 5. Psychometrics—methods. WM 141]
RC473.P78B37 2011
616.8′0475—dc22

2010044770

To Kenneth, Stephen, and Patricia, with love

About the Author

Russell A. Barkley, PhD, ABPP, is Clinical Professor of Psychiatry at the Medical University of South Carolina. Dr. Barkley has published numerous books, more than 200 scientific articles and book chapters, and 7 videos on ADHD and related disorders, including childhood defiance. He is also the editor of the newsletter *The ADHD Report.* A frequent conference presenter and speaker who is widely cited in the national media, he is past president of the Section on Clinical Child Psychology (the former Division 12) of the American Psychological Association, and of the International Society for Research in Child and Adolescent Psychopathology. His website is *www.russellbarkley.org.*

Acknowledgments

This manual and the construction of the Barkley Functional Impairment Scale (BFIS) would not have been possible without the assistance of others during the more than 16 years it has taken to develop, scientifically evaluate, and finally publish these latest versions of the scale. I am very appreciative of the assistance of my dear friend and colleague of more than 30 years, Mariellen Fischer, PhD, for her collaborative work with me on the longitudinal Milwaukee Study of hyperactive children followed into adulthood, frequently referenced throughout this manual. And I am especially grateful to my close friend and colleague of more than 20 years, Kevin R. Murphy, PhD, for his collaboration on numerous research projects we have conducted on adults with ADHD that served to inform the development of an earlier prototype of the BFIS and its initial validation. For the most recent summary of these extensive research programs, please see *ADHD in Adults: What the Science Says* (Barkley, Murphy, & Fischer, 2008). In addition, I wish to express my sincere appreciation to Wendy Mansfield and Sergei Rodkin of Knowledge Networks (Menlo Park, California) for their assistance with the collection of the data on the sample of U.S. adults used to create the norms for the BFIS in this manual. I further wish to acknowledge the support and encouragement of my wife of more than 40 years, Patricia Gann Barkley, throughout the research behind the rating scale and the preparation of this manual. Finally, I am indebted as always to my friends and colleagues at The Guilford Press, especially Kitty Moore, Seymour Weingarten, and Robert Matloff, for their acceptance, support of, and assistance with the normative project behind the BFIS and the publication of this manual.

RUSSELL A. BARKLEY, PhD

Contents

Introduction

The vast majority of mental disorders listed in the fourth edition (text revision) of the *Diagnostic and Statistical Manual of Mental Disorders* (DSM-IV-TR; American Psychiatric Association, 2000) require significant psychosocial impairment in major life activities as a separate criterion from the presence of significant symptoms for a diagnosis of a mental disorder. Establishing functional impairment in adult major life activities is also a significant component of various formal determinations of impairment and disability, such as those made under the Americans with Disabilities Act, by the Social Security Administration, by workers' compensation, and by other legal or official entities. However, definitions of the concept of "psychosocial impairment" remain vague and varied, and the domains it should include are often restricted to just three to five. Moreover, until now, there have been no assessment tools in this area that are reliable; are well validated; have norms based on a representative U.S. general population sample; and are commercially available for convenient use by clinicians, researchers, and industrial/organizational psychologists. The few instruments available to this point have been crude clinician ratings (such as the Global Assessment of Functioning Scale or the very similar Social and Occupational Functioning Assessment Scale in DSM-IV-TR), or a few patient self-report scales having a limited item pool and assessing a few domains of psychosocial functioning. Both approaches lack norms on a general population that would allow them to be used routinely for determining the degree to which self-reported impairment is statistically deviant or abnormal relative to impairment in that population. Several of the most commonly used rating systems are discussed briefly in this manual, but all are limited by this absence of normative information; limited coverage of psychosocial domains; and lack of availability for widespread clinical, research, and industrial/organizational use. The Barkley Functional Impairment Scale (BFIS) was developed to address this glaring need.

The BFIS has benefited from more than 16 years of research and development concerning the structure, reliability, validity, and utility of its item pool; its rating format; and evidence for its validity in evaluating possible impairment in major domains of psychosocial functioning in adults. The BFIS is an *empirically developed* scale—directly based on careful consideration of its domain content, on statistical analyses identifying its underlying dimensional nature and occurrence in adults, and on a large representative sample of the U.S. population (relative to 2000 U.S. Census information) that spans the life expectancy of most adults (ages 18–89 years).

Not only is the BFIS empirically based, reliable, and valid, but it is also exceptionally convenient to use. That is in large part because of the publisher's willingness to provide limited permission to reproduce the scales and score sheets for use by individual purchasers in their clinical or research practices. This will save the users much delay and inconvenience associated with the continual reordering of these items, as is commonplace in the scale-publishing industry.

This manual begins with a brief discourse on the nature of the concept of "psychosocial impairment" in Chapter 1. Subsequent chapters describe the developmental history, normative data, psychometric properties, and scoring/interpretation of the BFIS scales. The Appendix contains two long forms of the BFIS (BFIS-LF; both Self- and Other-Reports) for evaluating 15 major life activity domains for potential impairment. When time is of the essence in clinical, research, or administrative practices, the BFIS Quick Screen (both Self- and Other-Reports) can be used to gain a rapid determination of impairment in six major life activity domains often involved in disability determinations: self-care routines, home–chores, home–family, social–friends, education, and work. There is also a BFIS Impairment Interview form, which is very useful in conducting a recommended follow-up after a BFIS rating scale has been completed and scored, to obtain specific reasons why the informant (or significant other) may have rated a domain as at least moderately impaired or greater. Score sheets for the Self-Report versions of the BFIS-LF and BFIS Quick Screen contain tables of norms (percentiles) representative of the U.S. population. No normative data were collected for the Other-Report versions of these forms or for the Impairment Interview.

Without doubt, more research on the BFIS is desirable. Yet the information currently available suggests that the scores have satisfactory reliability, validity, and clinical utility for use in a variety of circumstances. These may include clinical practice settings with patients for whom concerns about impairment exist; research settings where the evaluation of impairment is of interest; treatment trials where a measure of response to intervention is needed; or industrial/organizational settings where the screening of adults for possible impairment is an important objective. I hope that you, my readers, will find the BFIS useful in screening and evaluating potential psychosocial impairment in major domains of adult life activities.

CHAPTER 1

Psychosocial Impairment

Definition and Assessment

Defining Impairment and Related Concepts

Impairment in psychosocial functioning is a requirement for the definition of the vast majority of mental disorders, and even for the determination of some disabilities due to both medical and mental disorders. The term "to impair" or "impairment" has been defined in various dictionaries as follows: "to cause to diminish, as in strength, value, or quality" (*medical-dictionary.thefreedictionary.com/impairment*); "a disability, any loss of physiological, psychological, or anatomical structure or function" (*Wikipedia.org*); "weakening, damage, or deterioration, especially as a result of injury or disease (*American Heritage Medical Dictionary*, 2009); "to make or cause to become worse; diminish in ability, value, excellence, etc.; weaken or damage" (*dictionary.reference.com*); "to damage or make worse by or as if by diminishing in some material respect" (*medical-dictionary.thefreedictionary.com/impairment*) or "a disorder in structure or function resulting from anatomic, physiologic, or psychologic abnormalities that interfere with normal activities" (*medical-dictionary.thefreedictionary.com/impairment*). The American Medical Association (2008) defines "impairment" as "a significant deviation, loss, or loss of use of any body structure or function in an individual with a health condition, disorder or disease." This definition and subsequent guidelines are often used in determining workers' compensation cases. Although DSM-IV-TR (American Psychiatric Association, 2000) provides no formal definition for the term "impairment," the phrase " . . . causes clinically significant distress or impairment in social, occupational, or other important areas of functioning" (p. 8) is attached to the diagnostic criteria for most mental disorders set forth in the manual. Explicit in the other definitions, yet only implied in the quotations given here, is that impairment is diminished functioning in important psychosocial domains of human life.

"Symptoms," in contrast, are defined as follows: "any sensation or change in bodily function that is experienced by a patient and is associated with a particular disease" (*wordnetweb.princeton.edu*); "a departure from normal function or feeling which is noticed by a patient, indicating the presence of disease or abnormality" (*Wikipedia.org*); "something that a patient experiences in his or her body that is different from what is normal, and that may be the result of a disease or its treatment" (*gemzar.com*); "a sign of a disease or dysfunction (or illness)" (*medical-dictionary.thefreedictionary.com/impairment*); or "a feeling, sensation, or experience associated with or resulting from a physical or mental disorder and noticeable by the patient" (*medical-dictionary.thefreedictionary.com/impairment*). A "symptom" is therefore a physical, cognitive, or behavioral manifestation of a disorder, whereas "impairment" refers to the consequences that arise from the expression of the disorder and its symptoms. These consequences usually include functional ineffectiveness in one or more major psychosocial domains of human life.

The term "disorder" is also variously defined in the literature. For instance, a "mental disorder" is defined in DSM-IV-TR (American Psychiatric Association, 2000) as "a clinically significant behavioral or psychological syndrome or pattern that occurs in an individual and that is associated with present distress (e.g., a painful symptom) or disability (i.e., impairment in one or more important areas of functioning) or with a significantly increased risk of suffering death, pain, disability, or an important loss of freedom" (p. xxxi). No attempt is made either to specify the underlying source or origin of this syndrome/pattern, or to indicate what would distinguish it from other patterns that might not be disorders. It misses, in other words, the essence of the concept of "disorder."

A widely considered and debated alternative view is provided by Wakefield (1992, 1997), who defines a "disorder" as a harmful dysfunction in an evolved mental or physical mechanism. He has borrowed the concept of "adaptation" (an evolved physical or mental mechanism) from the field of biology, and has made it the essence of the concept of "disorder": Disorders are dysfunctional adaptations. Medical disorders are failures or reductions of functioning in physical adaptations (such as organ systems), and mental disorders represent failures or diminutions in psychological functions (e.g., intelligence, memory, thinking/reasoning, visual–spatial abilities, language) or psychosocial functions (e.g., mobility, self-care, self-sufficiency/independence, social exchange/reciprocity, mating/pair bonding, childrearing, receptiveness to pedagogy/education). Adaptations are functional mechanisms that evolved to solve a problem in the environment of a species. Evolved adaptations are thus not trivial features or characteristics. They are biologically costly for an organism to develop and maintain, and so must serve some useful purpose; that is, the benefits of an adaptation must outweigh the costs to an individual for possessing that mechanism. The loss of, failure in, or reduction in functional effectiveness of an adaptation therefore often results in serious consequences for the individual—a reduced ability or inability to continue effectively addressing the adaptive problems the adaptation evolved to solve. When the mechanism can no longer effectively do this, the adaptive problems return, and the environment reacts with adverse consequences. Those consequences constitute the harm that may arise from such functional ineffectiveness.

Although the terms "impairment," "deficiency," "symptoms," "disability," and "disorder" are often used interchangeably in everyday conversation as well as in the medical, psychiatric, and psychological literatures, it is important not to confuse them. They represent separate components in the triadic sequence of events in reality—from the disorder to its symptoms (manifestations) to the functional impairment that ensues (ineffective performance and the harm that results). DSM-IV-TR (American Psychiatric Association, 2000) makes this distinction clear when it makes the requirement of impairment in major psychosocial activities a separate criterion for establishing the presence of a psychiatric disorder, apart from the presence of symptoms that result from or constitute the disorder. Impairment and symptoms are not identical either in their conceptualization or in reality. Research shows that severity of symptoms is only partially coupled to degree of impairment (Gordon et al., 2006; Lewandowski, Lovett, & Gordon, 2009). In other words, the extent of impairment does not have a perfect, direct relationship to the severity of symptoms, but is only partially predicted by that severity. This makes it clear that other factors besides symptoms alone contribute to the eventual level of psychosocial impairment an individual may experience.

In short, it is fruitful to consider symptoms as the physical, cognitive, or behavioral manifestations of a disorder. Disorders are dysfunctions in physical or psychological (mental) adaptations that result in harm. Impairment represents functional ineffectiveness—the inability to perform effectively in major domains of human life (adaptive problems)—and its harmful consequences. When an individual no longer functions effectively in addressing the everyday major adaptive problems of human life, the environment "kicks back" in ways that are costly or harmful to the individual. Functional ineffectiveness in major life activities (adaptive domains), resulting in adverse consequences, is therefore at the heart of the concept of impairment.

In this view, impairment not only refers to functional ineffectiveness in addressing the major adaptive problems of human life; it also refers to the harm that this functional ineffectiveness creates for an individual. A reduction in functional effectiveness that leads to no harm whatsoever in the absence of any accommodations, treatment, or habilitation is a trivial if not nonexistent form of impairment. In other words, "no harm, no foul." "Harm" in this definition typically refers to either increased risk for mortality, increased risk for morbidity (physical injury), or a significant adverse decline in functioning in a particular *major* human life activity (self-care, self-protection, self-sufficiency, social interaction, sexual relations, education, occupation, etc.). A "major life activity" in this perspective is one of the important adaptive domains that are largely or entirely universal to all mature humans and are necessary to their ability to sustain their survival, see to their welfare, and hence increase their long-term happiness (freedom from want or dissatisfaction). When the degree of dysfunction in an adaptation reaches a certain level, an individual may not be able to perform a major activity of daily life as well as the average, typical, or normal human; that is, the person has become significantly less effective. This ineffectiveness begins to have adverse consequences for the individual. Harm begins to accrue. Both the reduction in functional effectiveness and the attendant harm are regarded as the essence of the concept of impairment. The adverse consequences can even serve as a gauge to the degree of functional ineffectiveness—the degree of one's impairment.

A common element in various views on impairment is that the "normal" or "average" person serves as the standard against which the degree of functional ineffectiveness and attendant harm is to be judged (Gordon & Keiser, 1998). This is implied if not explicitly stated in the foregoing definitions of the terms "disorder" and "impairment." It has also been made explicit in the U.S. government's definition of the term "disability"—a term often used synonymously with "impairment." The Americans with Disabilities Act (ADA; Public Law 101-336, 1990) refers to a "disability" as "an inability to function normally, physically or mentally." (It goes on to describe a disability as an "inability to engage in any substantial gainful activity by reason of any medically determinable physical or mental impairment which can be expected to last or has lasted for a continuous period of not less than 12 months," and as "a physical or mental impairment that substantially limits one or more of the major life activities of [an] individual, a record of such an impairment, or being regarded as having such an impairment.") The Equal Employment Opportunity Commission, which is responsible for issuing regulations in regard to the ADA, has offered this clarification: "An individual is not substantially limited in a major life activity if the limitation does not amount to a significant restriction when *compared with the abilities of the average person*" (emphasis added). Similarly, impairment or disability is "the inability to function in the normal or usual manner" (*medical-dictionary.thefreedictionary.com/impairment*). The normal, typical, or average person in the general population—not some highly intelligent, high functioning, highly specialized, or highly educated peer group—is thus the standard against which impairment is judged.

With these ideas as a background, this manual takes as its starting point that "impairment" begins with a loss or diminution in the functional effectiveness of human physical or mental adaptations. It views this functional ineffectiveness as often being dimensional, not categorical, in nature; that is, there can be degrees of diminution in the functioning of most physical or mental adaptations, as opposed to all-or-none effectiveness. When an individual's ineffective functioning reaches such a magnitude that it begins to result in an inability to adapt to (solve) problems in the major domains of human life, adverse consequences arise for that individual (i.e., harm ensues). At that point or threshold, the person may be said to be impaired, disordered, or disabled.

This manual and the BFIS focus on the uppermost level of the trilevel hierarchy of impairment (physical, cognitive-behavioral, psychosocial)—the psychosocial arena of functional effectiveness. This is because the principal focus of the BFIS is on evaluating impairment in the context of psychiatric disorders or psychological problems, although it may also be of use in evaluating psychosocial impairment related to medical disorders. The major domains of human psychosocial life are likely to comprise the adaptive problems that some physical organs (the human brain) and most cognitive-behavioral adaptations evolved to address. It is probably at this level of adaptive problem solving where evolution (natural selection) has acted in the history of the species to create the lower-level cognitive-behavioral and even neurological adaptations.

As noted above, the normal, average, or typical human serves as the standard for judging functional ineffectiveness and its harmful consequences. To make such a determination, there must be information on the normal or general population against which an individual's reports can be compared. In other words, there must be norms available to assist with this judgment of impairment. That is one purpose of this manual: to provide normative information on the degree of functional ineffectiveness experienced (self-reported) by a representative sample of the adult general population in the performance of most major psychosocial domains of life activities.

Guidelines for Assessing Impairment or Disability

It is not the purpose of this manual to set forth detailed guidelines for the clinical evaluation of disorders and impairment. The American Medical Association, the American Psychiatric Association, the American Academy of Child and Adolescent Psychiatry, and the American Academy of Pediatrics, among others, have published detailed practice standards that should be consulted for such information. Yet a brief summary of two sets of official guidelines can be helpful in providing an overview of the essential or basic structure of such an evaluation.

Guidelines of the American Medical Association

The medical model of evaluation of disorders and their impairments has been set forth in the United States by the American Medical Association (2008), as represented in Table 14-4 of its guidelines (p. 352). That table lists specific suggestions to address in conducting a mental and behavioral disorders examination. These recommendations include the following:

- Screen an individual for past and current substance abuse, to determine whether symptoms of substance abuse better account for psychiatric symptoms.
- Evaluate the person's legal history, especially concerning prior lawsuits, work-related injuries, bankruptcies, incarcerations, driving while intoxicated, restraining orders, and court-ordered child support.
- Obtain the person's military history, including overseas service, adjustment to service, discharge history, pay grade, military arrests, and disability pension.
- Note whether there is a pattern of overendorsing symptoms during the psychiatric interview.
- Assess the patient's motivation for returning to work.
- Determine whether symptom exaggeration or malingering is present.
- Ask about the patient's attitude to the third-party payer (employer, insurance company, etc.).
- Assess the influence of the litigation process on return to work.
- Determine whether adequate pharmacological and biological treatment has been provided, including whether the patient has accepted and complied with reasonable treatment.

Although these recommendations are helpful at a broad or general level, the judgments of impairment made by following these criteria and associated ratings have poor interrater reliability (Leclair, Leclair, & Brigham, 2009).

The American Medical Association guidelines for mental disorders specify six areas of functional impairment for review in this evaluation: self-care and personal hygiene; social and recreational activities; the capacity for travel, including driving and using public transportation; interpersonal relationships; the capacity for concentration, persistence, and pace; and employability. Five of these are psychosocial, and one, interestingly, is cognitive-behavioral (the capacity for concentration, persistence, and pace). In determining the presence of impairment, the evaluator is encouraged to review information from other reliable sources, such as records from inpatient hospitalization, outpatient treatment, day treatment programs, occupational therapy, work evaluations, and disability assessments. The patient's self-reports of symptoms and their impact on these six functional areas, along with the information gathered from these sources and the findings from the objective clinical examination, are to be analyzed by the examiner in making a judgment of impairment or disability. Any wide disparities or incongruities between the patient's self-reports and the other sources of information, including the clinical evaluation, should be scrutinized to determine the reasons for these disparities. (For a more detailed discussion of the American Medical Association guidelines, see Leclair et al., 2009.)

Guidelines of the Social Security Administration

In the United States, the Social Security Administration (2008; see also *www.ssa.gov*) has issued guidelines for the determination of work-related disability, which must be total and permanent, not partial or temporary. The individual must be unable to do the work he/she did before; the person must be unable to adjust to other work because of the medical condition; and the disability must be expected to last at least 1 year or to result in death. The evaluation of disability on the basis of a mental disorder requires sufficient evidence to (1) establish the presence of "medically determinable mental impairment(s)," (2) assess the degree of functional limitation the impairment or impairments impose, and (3) project the probable duration of the impairment(s). Generally, the examiner is encouraged to follow the American Medical Association guidelines as described above in making the determination of medically determinable mental impairment(s).

In the criteria for the guidelines concerning disability due to mental disorders, the presence of a mental disorder must result in limitations in one or more of four functional domains:

1. *Activities of daily living.* These include adaptive activities such as cleaning, shopping, cooking, taking public transportation, paying bills, maintaining a residence, caring appropriately for personal grooming and hygiene, using telephones and directories, and using a post office.

2. *Social functioning at work or in personal life.* This includes the capacity to interact independently, appropriately, effectively, and on a sustained basis with other

individuals. Social functioning includes the ability to get along with others, such as family members, friends, neighbors, grocery clerks, landlords, or bus drivers. A person may demonstrate impaired social functioning by, for example, a history of altercations, evictions, firings, fear of strangers, avoidance of interpersonal relationships, or social isolation. He/she may exhibit strength in social functioning by such things as the ability to initiate social contacts with others, communicate clearly with others, or interact and actively participate in group activities. The examiner also needs to consider cooperative behaviors, consideration for others, awareness of others' feelings, and social maturity. Social functioning in work situations may involve interactions with the public, appropriate responses to persons in authority (e.g., supervisors), or cooperative behaviors involving coworkers.

3. *Concentration, persistence, and pace in completing tasks that are commonly part of work.* These are described as the ability to sustain focused attention and concentration sufficiently long to permit the timely and appropriate completion of tasks commonly found in work settings. Limitations in concentration, persistence, or pace are best observed in work settings, but may also be reflected by limitations in other settings.

4. *Decompensation or deterioration in work or work-like settings that may result in withdrawal from that situation or experiencing an exacerbation of symptoms,* as manifested by difficulties in performing activities of daily living, maintaining social relationships, or maintaining concentration, persistence, or pace. Episodes of decompensation may be demonstrated by an exacerbation in symptoms or signs that would ordinarily require increased treatment or a less stressful situation (or a combination of the two). Episodes of decompensation may be inferred from medical records showing significant alteration in medication; from documentation of the need for a more structured psychological support system (e.g., hospitalizations, placement in a halfway house, or a highly structured and directing household); or from other relevant information in the record about the existence, severity, and duration of the episode.

As in the American Medical Association guidelines, one domain is clearly cognitive-behavioral in nature (concentration, persistence, and pace). The other three are psychosocial (activities of daily living, social functioning, and work or employability).

Important to note in both these sets of guidelines is that the examiner is to analyze the patient's self-reports of symptoms and their impact on the four or six functional domains, to determine how consistent this information is with that obtained from the other sources. This is fine—but nowhere in either set is there any consideration of comparing a patient's self-reports against those of a general population sample to determine the extent to which the patient's reports are normal, typical, or deviant (abnormal). This raises the question of just how much typical, average, or normal people consider themselves to be functioning effectively or ineffectively (impaired) in these psychosocial domains. The answer is that until now, no one has really known; it has been left to clinicians to make that determination. But on what are clinicians relying in doing so? Besides their training and experience, most likely the reports of their patients. That may explain why the results of such evaluations are often found to be unreliable across examiners (Leclair et al., 2009). None of the other sources of information to be consulted in an examination provide that type of normative information, either. The American Psychiatric Association (Pincus et al., 1991) studied the consistency of the Social Security Administration guidelines against the actual statutory requirements for being declared disabled in the legislation related to Social Security Disability Insurance, and it gave a number of recommendations for improving the guidelines. However, none of these involved collecting normative information from the general population on the extent of its self-reported impairment in these psychosocial domains.

This is not to say that some structured methods for evaluating psychosocial impairment have not been used previously in the research literature on the subject. Several certainly have; however, none of them were given to a large sample of the general U.S. population to determine the extent to which this population would have self-reported various degrees of functional impairment in specific psychosocial domains. Only a sampling of the methods can be considered here, but they are typical of the rest.

Methods for Evaluating Psychosocial Impairment

Clinician Ratings

Of the four commonly used clinician ratings for determining the presence of psychosocial impairment to be considered here, the one most often cited is the Global Assessment of Functioning (GAF) Scale set forth in the current version of the DSM—at this writing, DSM-IV-TR (American Psychiatric Association, 2000, p. 34). The clinician giving this relatively simple rating on a single scale from 0 to 100 is to "consider psychological, social, and occupational functioning on a hypothetical continuum of mental health–illness," but is not to include "impairment . . . due to physical (or environmental) limitations." To understand this hypothetical continuum, consider what the lowest rating of 10 represents: **"Persistent danger of severely hurting self or others** (e.g., recurrent violence) **OR persistent inability to maintain minimal personal hygiene OR serious suicidal act with clear expectation of death"** (p. 34; bold in original). Contrast this with what the highest rating of 100 represents: **"Superior functioning in a wide range of activities, life's problems never seem to get out of hand, is sought out by others because of his or her many positive qualities. No symptoms"** (p. 34; bold in original).

Although the intent of the GAF Scale is laudable—that is, to provide clinicians with at least some guidance in making a judgment of the degree to which a mental disorder is associated with impairment—several problems exist with such a simple global judgment. Not the least of these have been repeated findings of low interjudge agreement on the scaling in the absence of training. The scale also does not distinguish among various major domains of psychosocial functioning, consistent with the American Medical Association and Social Security Administration guidelines. And so it cannot be made clear just what the specific nature of the impairment is, or, more precisely, in what domains of life the impairment is occurring. Lower ratings appear to represent not just more severe but more pervasive impairment across multiple domains. Yet the nature of these domains is unclear. Just as important is the lack of any information on just how the general population would be rated on such a scale, which would serve as a critical benchmark for determining what is normal or average for adult humanity, or at least adults in the United States. If a clinician has no information on how the general population would fare on such a scale, then the reliability (and hence validity) of such judgments will surely be limited.

A clinician rating scale related to the GAF Scale is the more focused Social and Occupational Functioning Assessment Scale (SOFAS), which is provided in an appendix to DSM-IV-TR for further study (American Psychiatric Association, 2000, p. 818). The instructions direct the clinician to "consider social and occupational functioning on a continuum from excellent functioning to grossly impaired functioning." In contrast to the GAF Scale, the SOFAS admonishes the clinician to "include impairments in functioning due to physical limitations, as well as those due to mental impairments." This proposed scale can be illustrated by what its lowest rating of 10 represents: "Persistent inability to maintain minimal personal hygiene. Unable to function without harming self or others or without considerable external support (e.g., nursing care and supervision)." Its highest rating of 100 reflects this: "Superior functioning in a wide range of activities."

A study on the construct validity of the SOFAS (Patterson & Lee, 1995) found that its scores were independent of Axis I, Axis II, and psychoactive substance dependence diagnoses, suggesting that it is assessing a construct apart from general psychopathology. This is a good thing not only for the construct of impairment, but also for the requirement in DSM-IV-TR that impairment be a separate criterion for establishing a diagnosis of a mental disorder from the specific symptom criteria. If impairment was simply another form of psychopathology, this requirement would be moot. The study by Patterson and Lee (1995) also found that six factors appeared to contribute to these ratings, accounting for nearly 52% of the variance in the ratings: patients' access to and use of transportation; medication compliance; number of agency referrals; current living situation; current potential for violence; and degree of social support. Though it is clear that the SOFAS (and probably the GAF Scale, on which it is based) is capturing a global construct of impairment, the same limitations are inherent in both scales. Again, the lack of information on the functioning of the general population throws clinicians back on their own limited experience and training in this regard, and hence their judgments have limited reliability and validity.

Another clinician rating scale is the Sheehan Disability Scale (DISS; Sheehan, 1983), although it can also be completed directly by the patient. The scale consists of three global domains or items, with each rated 0–10 in degree of impairment (the anchor points are not at all [0], mild [1–3], moderate [4–6], marked [7–9], and extreme [10]). The three domains on the DISS are work/school, social/leisure, and family life/home. Scores of 5 or higher are said to be worth clinical attention, as they are more likely to be associated with impairment. The DISS also asks about (1) how many days an individual missed school or work due to his/her symptoms or was to carry out normal daily responsibilities; and (2) how many days his/her productivity was reduced by the symptoms even if the person went to school or work. The scale seems to have been created specifically for evaluating people with panic, phobic, other anxiety, or depressive symptoms. But a subsequent paper by the developer (Sheehan, Harnett-Sheehan, & Raj, 1996) presented results for other psychiatric disorders, suggesting that the DISS could be extended for use beyond patients with anxiety or mood symptoms. The scale can be completed in 1–2 minutes by either a patient or a clinician. It has been used in psychopharmacology research and seems to be sensitive to treatment effects (Leon, Shear, Portera, & Klerman, 1992; Sheehan et al., 1996). An analysis of some of the scale's psychometric properties found satisfactory internal consistency (.56–.74 at first administration) and a single-factor structure, suggesting a general impairment dimension underlying the specific item domains of work/school, social/leisure, and family life/home (Leon et al., 1992).

Sheehan and colleagues (1996) cited their own work and that of others indicating that severity of symptoms was only partially coupled with severity of disability (impairment) on the DISS: Not all disorders resulted in disability, and not everyone with a particular disorder received a score indicating disability on the scale. This partial decoupling of severity of symptoms from severity of impairment would be noted again in the field of attention-deficit/hyperactivity disorder (ADHD) 10 years later (Gordon et al., 2006). Also, treatments that reduced symptoms did not necessarily result in corresponding decreases in disability. Thus symptoms did not equate directly with disability (impairment), as the authors noted. The 1996 study also reported that disability scores in 102 psychiatric inpatients increased with age among patients, as well as among those with higher education. Higher scores were found among those who were widowed, separated, or divorced than among those who were living in a "family situation." No relationship was found for gender or age of onset of disorder, but number of prior hospitalizations was linked to increased current disability scores.

As with the GAF Scale and the SOFAS, no normative information exists for the DISS concerning the degree of impairment that would be found in a general population sample. This makes it difficult to judge whether the ratings provided by either the clinician or the patient on this scale are actually deviant relative to the reports that would be given by the average or normal person. Yet comparison to normative information on the general population is essential to the determination of impairment, as it is inherent in its very definition.

The Psychiatric Impairment Rating Scale (PIRS; Parmegiani, Lovell, Skinner, & Milton, 2001) is yet another means by which a clinician rating of impairment due to a psychiatric disorder can be obtained. The PIRS asks about functioning in various domains of major life activities that are very similar to those stipulated in the Social Security Administration and American Medical Association guidelines: self-care and hygiene; social and recreational; travel; social function; concentration, persistence, and pace; and employability. This should not be surprising, since these are the domains contained in the Workcover legislation for New South Wales, which were modeled on the Social Security Administration guidelines in the United States and are consistent with the American Medical Association guidelines. The PIRS was developed for the New South Wales Motor Accidents Authority in Australia and is also used in other Australian states. However, its validity and coverage as a measure of impairment associated with psychiatric disorders have been questioned by

Australian mental health professional groups, such as the Australian Psychological Association (see Davies, 2008).

The PIRS is made up of six scales, each designed to evaluate a specific area of functional impairment. The six functional impairment scales are each scored with a 5-point, anchored scale. The two *middle* scores (of the six) are summed and translated to a percentage of impairment from 0% to a maximum of 50%. Evidence suggests that this restriction in the ratings results in reduced correlations with other measures and significantly biases the assessed disability in a downward direction (Davies, 2008). Although this scale has high content or face validity, it lacks empirical evidence to support other forms of validity, such as construct, divergent, and criterion validity (Bryant, 2000). These limitations undermine its use as a measure of impairment (Davies, 2008). Correlations among the scale items suggest that the domains of employability; concentration, persistence, and pace; social and recreational; and self-care and hygiene probably form a single factor. The social function domain is less related to these other domains and may represent a separate smaller factor.

Yet another clinician-rated scale for assessing psychosocial impairment as a function of psychiatric disorder is the Longitudinal Interval Follow-up Evaluation—Range of Impaired Functioning Tool (LIFE-RIFT; Leon et al., 1999). This is a semistructured interview that evaluates four domains of psychosocial functioning: work, interpersonal relations, recreation, and global satisfaction. In each domain, impairment is rated on a 1–5 scale (1–2 = no impairment, 3 = mild, 4 = moderate, 5 = severe; 0 = not applicable, 6 = no information). The work domain actually subsumes three more specific domains (employment, home, and student); the interpersonal relations domain refers specifically to spouse, children, other relatives, and friends. Global satisfaction and recreation are not broken down further. Factor analysis reveals a single-factor solution (Leon et al., 1999). Internal consistency of the scale is satisfactory (Cronbach's alpha = .82). The scale has reasonable stability (intraclass correlations of .55–.61), has high interrater reliability ($r = .94$), and is sensitive to and predictive of recovery 6 months later (Leon et al., 1999). It not only readily distinguished depressed from normal control groups in one study, but was even sensitive to the level (severity) of depressive episodes (Judd et al., 2000). Although most of the research on the LIFE-RIFT has been done with depression, studies have also shown its utility with anxiety disorders (Warshaw, Keller, & Stout, 1994) and adult ADHD (Safren, Sprich, Cooper-Vince, Knouse, & Lerner, 2010). The study by Safren and colleagues (2010) indicated that adult ADHD was chiefly associated with work impairment ratings and, to a lesser degree, ratings of impaired interpersonal relations. The interpersonal relations and global satisfaction domains were associated with depression, while global satisfaction was associated with anxiety.

Several problems are immediately evident with all of these clinician-based rating methods for evaluating psychosocial impairment. First, the range of major life activity domains they cover is seriously restricted: They address mainly the domains of self-care; work or employability; social functioning; and concentration, persistence, and pace. This is understandable, given the focus of some clinician rating systems on the determination of work-related disability, as in the American Medical Association and Social Security Administration guidelines. A few systems also address travel (mobility) and recreation. It is not clear why the domain of recreation would be considered a significant domain of human impairment separate from social functioning. Nor is it evident why concentration is considered a major domain of psychosocial functioning; rather, it is an important cognitive ability, especially for productive work. Yet if one is concerned more broadly with the range of major domains of life activities in which humans engage (especially in developed countries), then financial management, sexual behavior and relations, participation in organized community activities (church, clubs, organizations, sports, societies, etc.), marriage/cohabiting/dating, childrearing, driving, and health maintenance, among others, should probably be included. Education is also a major life activity—for young adults, obviously, but increasingly for adults of all ages still participating in the work force. This is so because of demands for ongoing adult education as part of many occupations, as well as retraining in new occupations or specialties for career advancement or reemployment after layoff. Yet the domain of education is not mentioned in any of these clinician rating systems.

Second, the range of possible ratings is often relatively truncated (a 4- or 5-point scale). As Davies (2008) has noted for the PIRS, limiting the range of rated impairment may restrict the range of correlations a scale is likely to have with other impairment measures. It may also result in a bias toward a rather low threshold for establishing the presence of impairment or disability.

Third, nationally normative data are not available to determine the extent to which the ratings on these methods would be distributed in a general population sample. Such information is indispensable to comparing an individual's rated level of impairment to the level typically reported by or assigned to the general, average, or normal population. If the "average person" standard is to serve as the benchmark for establishing someone as clinically significantly impaired, then information about that "average person" (the general population distribution) needs to be available. This is also important, given that the clinician rating relies heavily upon and so is significantly correlated with the patient-reported severity of symptoms and impairments (Davies, 2008). As a source of information about degree of impairment, a clinician rating is thus not really independent from a patient self-report; rather, it is chiefly a proxy for those self-reports, filtered through the experience, training, and even biases of the clinician doing the rating.

A fourth problem, as Davies (2008) has noted in critiquing the PIRS, is that no information has been presented for these methods to show that domain ratings by clinicians have any validity. Researchers must establish the validity of these ratings by demonstrating relationships to other measures of impairment in those same domains. For example, ratings of functioning at work must show relationships to work history, adverse events in occupational functioning, archival records (e.g., days worked, days absent, sick leave, or workers' compensation claims), employer ratings of job performance, and so on.

Patient Self-Ratings of Psychosocial Impairment

Several patient-completed rating scales exist for the evaluation of psychosocial impairment. One is the Impairment Rating section of the Patient Mood Chart

(PMC; Parker, Tully, Olley, & Barnes, 2007). A patient completes this scale daily, using a 0–3 Likert scale to rate the degree to which his/her depression impaired functioning in three domains: (1) work; (2) interactions with colleagues, family, and friends; and (3) ability to get things done. Parker and colleagues (2007) found that the PMC Impairment Rating correlated –.53 with the SOFAS (see above) and with other measures of depression and anxiety. Given that the clinician-rated SOFAS is largely driven by the patient's self-reports, such a correlation between the patient self-rating on the PMC and the SOFAS is not surprising. It is relatively weak evidence for validity. Certainly more evidence than this for the validity and utility of this measure is desirable.

Another patient-completed rating scale is the Clinical Impairment Assessment (CIA; Bohn et al., 2008). This is a 16-item rating scale in which each item is rated on a 0–3 Likert scale for frequency of difficulties (0 = not at all, 3 = a lot). It is intended specifically for patients with an eating disorder, and it concerns the impact of their eating symptoms on their mood and self-perception, social functioning, and work functioning. Only the latter two domains would be placed in the arena of psychosocial functioning. The developers found that both a global single-factor solution and a three-factor solution (Personal, Cognitive, Social) worked to describe the scale's underlying dimensions. The CIA correlated well (.68) with clinician-rated psychosocial impairment and with the patient-completed Eating Disorders Questionnaire.

A relatively simple patient self-rating scale is the Work and Social Adjustment Scale (WSAS; Mundt, Marks, Swear, & Griest, 2002). This is a short 5-item rating of degree of impairment secondary to a disorder that is to be specified by the clinician or researcher. The items can be presented and recorded over the telephone, using digitized voice recordings of instructions and items and a touch-tone keypad telephone. Each item is rated on a 0–8 Likert scale for degree of impairment in that domain. The specific domains to be rated are work, managing a home, social leisure, private leisure, and ability to form and maintain close relationships. The initial study of the scale found acceptable test–retest reliability (.73) and internal consistency (.79–.81). The scale correlated .76 with the Hamilton Depression Scale and .81 with clinician-rated impairment. Factor analysis in two separate studies (involving patients with depression and obsessive–compulsive disorder, respectively) revealed a single underlying factor consistent with other scales evaluating psychosocial impairment.

The self-report scale of impairment most relevant to this manual is the Impairment Rating Scale (IRS), part of an adult ADHD rating scale used in our earlier research (Barkley & Murphy, 1998, 2006). The IRS served as the prototype for the BFIS (see Chapter 2). It contained 10 domains of major life activities, each rated on a 0–3 Likert scale (rarely or not at all, sometimes, often, and very often) to indicate the frequency with which an individual experienced impairment in these domains as a result of ADHD symptoms. The domains included home life; work; educational activities; social interactions; marriage and dating; leisure activities; driving; money management; community activities; and handling daily responsibilities. Individual ratings could be analyzed separately, but typically two scores were computed from this scale: (1) the Total Impairment Score, or the total of all domain ratings; and (2) the Percent Domains Impaired score, or the percentage of domains rated as being impaired (responses of often or very often—i.e., ratings of 2 or 3). The IRS was used in several studies of adults with ADHD and showed satisfactory divergent validity in discriminating adults with ADHD from Clinical control and Community control adults. It was also used in research on children with ADHD followed to adulthood whose ADHD persisted, compared to those with nonpersistent ADHD or a Community control group (Barkley et al., 2008). Interrater reliability (self- vs. other-reports) was satisfactory, and the ratings were associated with several other specific measures of impairment in these various domains, as well as with the clinician SOFAS rating.

It is certainly the case that self-report rating scales assessing quality of life (see Frisch, Cornell, Villaneuva, & Retzlaff, 1992, for an example) may overlap in their domain content with rating scales of impairment (work, recreation, social relationships, family, etc.). But the former scales are not evaluating the degree of functional ineffectiveness and harm being self-reported in these areas, which is the meaning of impairment. Instead, quality-of-life scales evaluate the extent of satisfaction, happiness, or well-being with these domains of life. Degree of happiness or satisfaction in any domain may be low, but this does not mean that individuals necessarily consider themselves as functioning ineffectively or being impaired or disabled in them.

Some of the same problems noted above for clinician ratings of psychosocial impairment also plague these and other patient rating scales. Although the range of major life activity domains appears to be broader on many of these scales, especially the 10-domain IRS, even these appear to miss some important domains of adult life (such as sexual behavior and relations, childrearing, and health maintenance). They may also cluster some domains into global categories, such as social functioning, rather than distinguishing among relations with family, with friends, and with strangers or acquaintances, for instance. In addition, the ranges of item ratings for many of these scales are restricted, as are those for many clinician rating systems; this restriction creates artificially low relationships with other measures of impairment in those domains. Moreover, little if any information is available on just how valid the individual domain ratings are in capturing actual impairment in each domain, as judged by other methods or sources for evaluating that domain. For instance, do those who rate themselves as impaired in work actually have other evidence for such impairment that correlates with this domain rating? Showing that ratings of impairment are distinct from ratings of psychopathological symptoms, as many of these scales have done, is fine as one source of evidence for the validity of impairment as a distinct construct from psychopathology. But it is not sufficient evidence of construct, discriminant, or criterion validity. Furthermore, these scales, like the clinician rating methods, lack normative information on a nationally representative sample of adults that would permit some determination of the position of these self-ratings within the larger distribution of self-rated impairment in a general population sample. For this reason, these rating scales cannot be used in clinical practice or other settings for the evaluation of impairment in patients or for other purposes in which the issue of psychosocial impairment is exceptionally important.

Suggestions for Assessing Psychosocial Impairment

As suggested by the American Medical Association and others, the clinical assessment of psychosocial impairment in adults should typically include the following:

- An initial interview to determine the nature of the impairments, the major life domains in which they may be occurring, and the symptoms/disorders that may be giving rise to them.
- A careful history of the patient's symptoms, other concerns, medically relevant information, and prior evaluations for and treatments received for these same complaints.
- A determination of the developmental inappropriateness of the symptoms, relative to those reported by members of the general population.
- Establishing the age of onset and course of the impairments and relevant disorders to date.
- A physical exam, if functional impairment is thought to have arisen from a medical disorder.
- Psychological testing, if general cognitive ability, academic achievement, or specific neuropsychological abilities are believed to be affected and contributing to impairment in psychosocial functioning.
- Ruling in or out other treatable medical and psychiatric disorders that may be contributing to the clinical presentation, symptoms, and impairments that are concerns of the patient.
- Reviewing the available archival records related to particular domains of psychosocial impairment that may be of key importance to the purpose of the evaluation (work-related records, official driving records, official criminal records, educational transcripts or report cards, prior medical records related to disability determinations, prior medical and psychiatric evaluation and treatment records, military records, etc.).
- Corroborating the self-reports of psychosocial impairment (and symptoms) through the reports of others who know the patient well.
- *A determination of the degree of statistical deviance (abnormality) of the patient's self-reported impairment relative to that of the general population.*

This last source of information is not included in other guidelines for the evaluation of impairment or disability, but it is essential to establishing the position of the individual relative to the normal, average, or typical human (the average of the general population). After all, if impairment is to be judged in relation to the average person, as recommended by the ADA and as implied or explicit in various definitions of the term, then some means of comparing the individual's complaints about his/her psychosocial functioning to those given by the general population is indispensable to the determination of impairment.

An essential method for assessing most of these issues remains the clinical interview, of course. Behavior rating scales of psychiatric symptoms are also highly useful, but for initial screening for risk of disorders and for establishing the degree of developmental deviance (age-inappropriateness) of the patient's symptoms when mental disorders are believed to be the source of the functional impairment. Psychological testing may be useful as well in establishing the extent of cognitive-behavioral impairment, should that be a possible source of the difficulties experienced at the higher level of psychosocial impairment. And, as the American Medical Association makes plain, a physical examination is often essential to establish the presence of medical disorders that may also be contributing to psychosocial impairment. Until now, well-normed rating scales of functional impairment in major psychosocial domains were not widely available to permit clinicians to do likewise for the major life activities that may be functionally impaired by these symptoms and related mental or medical disorders. The BFIS was developed to fill that void. The BFIS is also exceptionally convenient for evaluating change in psychosocial impairment resulting from various interventions, such as medications or efforts at rehabilitation. In addition, it can be used to evaluate possible pre- to post-injury changes in psychosocial impairment status.

The Seven Sources of Information

As emphasized in the various governmental and professional guidelines for evaluating impairment, no single source of information can serve as the sole basis or "gold standard" for making the final determination of the existence and degree of psychosocial impairment. Seven types or sources of information are frequently needed in making such a determination:

- Patient self-reports of symptoms and impairments
- Patient-reported history of symptoms and impairments
- Psychological testing, where necessary
- Physical (medical) examinations, as appropriate
- Archival (official) records (the "paper trail" of impairment)
- Population norms for comparison to the self-reported symptoms and impairments
- Reports of significant others who know the patient well

Again, these last two sources and types of information are rarely if ever mentioned in guidelines for conducting evaluations of disability; however, they can provide valuable information to which the information obtained from the other sources can be compared, and vice versa. Indeed, the determination of the extent to which self-reported impairment compares to that provided by a general population sample would seem to be essential for this determination, as noted above.

Triangulating the Sources

A clinician should then engage in a process of triangulating these sources of information against each other and against the clinician's own training and experience in these matters, to arrive at a final determination of impairment. A useful metaphor for evaluating these different sources of information in arriving at a determination of impairment is the global positioning system (GPS) method. The GPS method triangulates one source of information about an individual's position against two or more other sources to arrive at a reasonably accurate report of the individual's geographical location on the planet. Likewise, a clinician should arrive at a patient's degree of impairment relative to that of the general population by comparing multiple sources of information about the patient against each other. Truth is an assembled thing, and this is certainly true in the area of impairment determination in clinical practice. Each source of information is judged against that provided by two others to gauge the integrity or validity of the initial source. And then this process is repeated across all seven of the domains listed above, so that all possible combinations of three-way comparisons are achieved. This process is more likely to lead the clinician to arrive at the most valid and reasonable approximation of reality—in this case, the individual's degree of psychosocial impairment.

Malingering

A major problem in disability or impairment determinations is the possibility of malingering. "Malingering" is defined in DSM-IV-TR as "the intentional production of false or grossly exaggerated physical or psychological symptoms, motivated by external incentives such as avoiding military duty, avoiding work, obtaining financial compensation, evading criminal prosecution, or obtaining drugs" (American Psychiatric Association, 2000, p. 739). There is a substantial literature on this issue that cannot be reviewed here (see Lovett, Gordon, & Lewandowski, 2009, for a more detailed discussion). Suffice to say that even the American Medical Association and Social Security Administration guidelines warn clinicians to evaluate the possibility that individuals are feigning the severity of their symptoms and impairments, usually for some personal gain.

There is no unequivocally guaranteed, foolproof means of detecting malingering. In the realm of psychological evaluations, one often sees "validity scales" included in such assessment methods as personality tests. In neuropsychology, "effort tests" may be given to trick a patient into believing that the test being given is one evaluating disability, when in fact it is being used to detect feigning. Whenever some obvious or external benefit is a possible result of the determination of impairment, clinicians should be alert to the possibility of malingering (Lovett et al., 2009). No single method of assessment can necessarily be free of the possibility of feigning or malingering, so no single approach can serve as a surefire means of detecting it. Probably the best means of detecting possible malingering is the method of triangulating sources of information against each other, discussed just above. When all possible combinations of three-way comparisons have been considered, a clinician can gain a more thorough perspective not only on the issue of impairment, but on the possibility of malingering. That is because it is rarely if ever possible for an individual to coordinate the data provided by all these sources so that they are consistent with and abet the scheme of misrepresentation.

Summary

This brief introduction to the nature and assessment of psychosocial impairment has argued for a distinction among the terms "symptom," "disorder," and "impairment/disability," so as to avoid confusion in readers' thinking and in their evaluation of the literature on these topics. Symptoms can be considered as the physical, cognitive, and behavioral manifestations of a disorder. They often form patterns or syndromes as described in DSM-IV-TR. Disorders are dysfunctions in physical or psychological (mental) adaptations that result in reducing or diminishing individuals' functional effectiveness in meeting the demands of daily life. Such ineffectiveness leads to harm. Impairment represents both this functional ineffectiveness in major domains of daily life activities *and* the harm resulting from it. Impairment is diminished functioning relative to that of the normal, average, or typical adult; it is *abnormal* in its degree, and thus must be judged relative to the "normal person" standard. Various guidelines exist for the determination of impairment, and various structured assessment tools have been developed for assisting with that determination (clinician ratings, patient self-ratings). But until now there has been little or no normative information available on the extent to which adults in the general population view themselves as being impaired in the major domains of life activities. Yet comparing an individual to this general population would seem to be an indispensable part of the larger process of assessing the individual's impairment. The BFIS was developed to address that void.

CHAPTER 2

Development of the BFIS

History, Survey Methods, and Normative Sample

This chapter describes the initial development of the BFIS, its final structure, and the methods used to collect information on the scale from a normative sample of U.S. adults ages 18–89 years.

Developmental History of the BFIS

The development of the BFIS began more than 16 years ago, in my initial studies at both the Medical College of Wisconsin (the Milwaukee Study, conducted with Mariellen Fischer, PhD) and the University of Massachusetts Medical Center (the UMASS Study, conducted with Kevin Murphy, PhD) on the extent of impairment experienced by adults with ADHD. The scale was originally created as a means (1) to quickly evaluate or screen adults presenting to our ADHD clinics for risk of psychosocial impairment secondary to ADHD; (2) to measure self-rated psychosocial impairment as part of our large-scale federally funded research grants on the nature of comorbidity and impairment associated with ADHD (see Barkley et al., 2008); and (3) to evaluate self-rated psychosocial impairment in hyperactive children (with ADHD) followed to adulthood (again, see Barkley et al., 2008). As described in Chapter 1, the early prototype scale, the Impairment Rating Scale (IRS), was embedded as a section within a larger rating scale assessing symptoms of adult ADHD. The IRS evaluated 10 domains of major life activities—home life; work; social interactions; community activities; educational activities; marriage and dating; money management; driving; leisure activities; and handling daily responsibilities—and provided a 4-point Likert scale (0–3) for responding to each domain. Respondents were simply asked to rate the degree of functional impairment they believed they were experiencing in these 10 domains as a result of their ADHD symptoms. Each domain was a single item, to be rated for frequency of problems as follows: rarely or not at all, sometimes, often, or very often (0–3, respectively). Although each rating could be studied separately, typically these numerical responses were summed to create a Total Impairment Score (see Chapter 6 and Barkley et al., 2008). The results could be compared to those for the different control groups being used in these projects, to determine degree of psychosocial impairment. Much of the research validating the BFIS was done with this earlier 10-domain prototype, the IRS, and this research is discussed in later chapters concerning reliability and validity information. But lacking until the present time was information on a nationally (U.S.) representative normative sample that would permit use of these impairment ratings in clinical, research, or industrial/organizational settings. Control groups are not available in such settings, as they are in research studies for making judgments about ratings' degree of statistical deviance.

To meet this need, the original IRS was pulled from its place inside the original ADHD rating scale, was expanded to include 10 additional domains initially, and was given a wider 0–9 Likert scale for responses in each domain. The original ascertainment window, however, was retained; that is, respondents were directed to consider their functioning during the prior 6 months in completing the scale items. Norms also needed to be collected on a large sample of adults that was representative of the U.S. general population. This manual presents those findings and norms based on 1,242 adults 18–89 years of age representative of the U.S. population, at least according to the 2000 U.S. Census (*www.census.gov*).

The new version of the scale, the BFIS, initially included the 10 domains from the IRS, along with the following 10 additional domains. The home life domain was separated into three more specific domains: completing home chores and managing a household; self-care routines; and home life with family. The social interactions domain was split into two separate, more specific domains: social relationships with friends, and social interactions with strangers and acquaintances. And new domains were added for childrearing, sexual activities and relations, health maintenance, caring for one's major items of property, obeying the law, avoiding the use of illegal substances, and controlling the use of legal substances. The domain of marriage and dating was clarified and broadened to include other intimate cohabiting relationships. As noted above, the response format for each domain was also expanded to a 10-point (0–9) Likert scale, to permit the determination of a wider range of functional impairment than was possible with the original IRS. An option was added to the response format for respondents to indicate that a particular domain did not apply to them (e.g., childrearing for individuals who were not parents, driving for those individuals who did not drive). Finally, instead of the response format for each item reflecting frequency of problems (rarely, sometimes, etc.), the anchor points for the 0–9 Likert scale were changed to reflect severity or degree of functional ineffectiveness or impairment in each domain (i.e., not at all, somewhat, mild, moderate, and severe).

Further review of the domain content of the first draft of the BFIS, along with statistical analyses, indicated that three of the new domains—those related to substance use (legal and illegal), as well as obeying the law—formed a separate factor from that containing the other domains. And two other domains—driving and childrearing—had loadings as high on this factor as on the first factor reflecting general impairment. This is not surprising, since both of these domains have elements of legal responsibilities and consequences associated with them. This result appeared to create a second factor concerning antisocial conduct (a form of psychopathology) besides the initial larger one of psychosocial impairment. And so the three domains related to legal substance use, illegal substance use, and obeying the law were removed from the final version of the BFIS. Also, discussions with colleagues suggested that 2 of the remaining 17 domains were clinically trivial and unlikely to be regarded by others as major domains of impairment in psychosocial activities. These domains were leisure activities and caring for one's major items of property. They were also among the weakest-loading domains on the psychosocial impairment factor. Therefore, to avoid trivializing the item pool of the BFIS these two domains were also removed from further consideration. This left a scale content of 15 domains believed to reflect the most important major life activities for most adults in the United States (and most developed countries).

As Chapter 1 has noted, an important issue here is just how the term "psychosocial impairment" is defined. For the BFIS, the following explicit written instructions were given to respondents in the normative sample, to guide them in judging how impaired they viewed themselves as being in each domain:

> How much difficulty do you have functioning effectively in each of these major life activities? That is, to what degree do you see yourself as being impaired in each of these life domains? Please circle the number next to each item that best describes your difficulties in functioning **DURING THE PAST 6 MONTHS**. If that situation does not apply to you (for instance, you don't drive a car, don't have children, don't live with anyone, etc.), please circle the 99 in the last column (under "Does not apply").

Here it is made evident that "impairment" means the degree of difficulty a person believes he/she experiences in functioning effectively in any psychosocial domain. Hence *degree of impairment refers to degree of functional ineffectiveness in a particular major life activity domain.* How much difficulty does a person have to report to be considered impaired, relative to the average person or normal human being in the U.S. population (the "average person" standard used in the ADA)? That question is addressed in Chapter 3, after an examination of the extent to which the normative sample responded with each of the possible 0–9 ratings for each of the 15 domains on the BFIS.

Normative information is *not* available for the Other-Report forms of the BFIS. Instead, these forms are used to evaluate what a patient reports against what someone who knows the person well reports. Information has been collected in prior research (Barkley, Knouse, & Murphy, in press) on the extent of such disparities in a clinical sample of adults with ADHD and two control samples. Such studies provide clinically important information about degree of self–other disparities when they become relatively large.

The BFIS items focus on rating the degree of functional impairment an individual believes he/she is experiencing in each psychosocial domain, rather than on positive or normative functioning. The BFIS was intended for clinical purposes—specifically, to be used to evaluate the range of functional impairment in clinic-referred or high-risk adults. In this situation, an examiner is faced with the question of the extent to which a clinical patient's complaints concerning his/her problems are indicative of impairment in psychosocial functioning from medical or mental disorders. The question here is how *typical or atypical* the patient's complaints are, rather than where a person falls within the distribution of normal variation in normal functioning in these various major life domains within the general population. In other words, the BFIS approaches the issue of impairment from the standpoint of deficit measurement.

Deficit measurement is typical in the development of clinical assessment devices, such as those used to assess anxiety disorders, mood disorders, or other adult psychological disorders. The distribution of such scores is quite different from the more typical bell-shaped curve of the distribution of normal variation in a typical psychological ability, such as intelligence or academic achievement. The score distribution of a deficit measurement tool can be expected to have a highly skewed distribution toward the zero point or lowest score on the scale, with a steep dropoff in the percentage of the general population that manifests an increasing degree of impairment. Deficit assessment evaluates the likelihood that a patient's complaints are sufficiently severe or numerous as to place these significantly outside the distribution of typical complaints for the general population. This is the purpose of the BFIS: It is a deficit measurement method, not a test of normal variation in a human ability. Hence its instructions direct respondents to report their degree of functional difficulties; it does not attempt to assess the range of normal abilities in each of these 15 domains.

It is very important to note here that the BFIS contains instructions to rate the degree of functional impairment *without reference to any specific mental or medical disorder*. In this manner, degree of impairment can be established separately from the presence or absence of such a disorder. This permits the BFIS to be used as part of the evaluation of *any* medical or mental disorder that could lead to difficulties in psychosocial functioning in these 15 domains. Determining the cause(s) of the psychosocial impairment is a separate issue involving differential diagnosis. If a disorder such as ADHD, an anxiety or mood disorder, or a neurological or general medical disorder were specified in the instructions of the rating scale, it would be applicable only to patients known to have that disorder. This would limit the applicability and value of the scale, as a patient might rate only the degree of impairment related to that disorder and not the overall degree of impairment generally.

Methods for Collecting the Normative Sample

The 15-domain BFIS was then given to a nationally representative sample of adults in the United States ages 18–70+. The survey company contracted to obtain this national sample was instructed to ensure that equal representation of males and females occurred in each of six age groups for each of nine regions representing the United States. The company chosen for this task was Knowledge Networks of Menlo Park, California (see *knowledgenetworks.com* for more information on the company).

Knowledge Networks conducted the survey by using the Web-enabled Knowledge Panel, a probability-based panel designed to be representative of the U.S. population. Initially, participants were chosen scientifically by a random selection of telephone numbers and residential addresses. Persons in selected households are then invited by telephone or by mail to participate in the Knowledge Panel. For those who agreed to participate but did not already have Internet access, Knowledge Networks provided at no cost a laptop and Internet service provider connection. This was very important, as surveying only people who already had computers and Internet connections would immediately have biased the sample away from one that was representative of the U.S. population. People who already had computers and Internet service were permitted to use their own equipment to participate. Panelists then received unique log-in information for accessing surveys online, and then were sent emails throughout each month inviting them to participate in research. Panelists were paid for their completion of the survey. More technical information is available on the website mentioned above (*www.knowledgenetworks.com/ganp/reviewer-info.html*).

The Self-Report version of the 15-domain BFIS was provided to Knowledge Networks as a rating scale in which respondents were to answer each item on a 10-point Likert scale (0–9), with anchor points for rating degree of impairment or difficulties in functioning ranging from not at all (0) to somewhat (1, 2), mild (3, 4), moderate (5–7), and severe (8, 9). The scale was uploaded to an Internet site, and members of the Knowledge Panel were invited to complete them. The Other-Report forms and the Impairment Interview version were not used in this study. The survey was conducted in April 2010 and was completed within 3 weeks of the initial invitation. The company was contracted to obtain completed scales on at least 1,200 adults divided into six age groups (18–29, 30–39, 40–49, 50–59, 60–69, and 70+), with at least 100 males and 100 females in each age group. A final sample of 1,249 adults was obtained. A small subset of 62 participants (31 males and 31 females) were invited to complete the survey a second time, 2–3 weeks after the initial scale was completed, to provide information for computing test–retest reliability.

Knowledge Networks requires that participants be given the option of choosing not to answer a question. For most BFIS questions (domains), this did not occur; however, for some questions, a rare participant did refuse to answer. For each of the questions for which refusals occurred, this occurred between 1 and 34 times, with an average of 12 such refused replies for such questions. This constituted a refusal rate of 0–2.7% for those items on which this occurred, averaging a 0.9% refusal rate. In these rare cases, the missing answer was replaced with 99 (does not apply), so that the remaining data for this participant could be used in the project. This practice was based on the argument that this would create a conservative bias in the responses to that item. Instances where respondents reported that a domain did not apply to them were coded as missing data.

It is important to note here that this sample was not subsequently filtered to remove individuals who had a prior history of psychiatric diagnosis; who were currently being treated with psychiatric medications; or who might have learning, developmental, neurological, or medical disorders. Such filtering has occurred in collecting normative information for other scales. However, doing so creates a supernormal comparison group, not a general population sample, and can result in impairments being found at far lower levels of deviance on the ratings than would be the case if a general population sample free of such filtering had been used. The BFIS was based on just such an unfiltered general population sample, so that individual impairment scores on it could be compared to the "average person" standard so important in the definition of the term "impairment" (see Chapter 1).

Demographic Characteristics of the National Sample

As noted above, a total of 1,249 adults completed the survey. The sample sizes for each age group by sex are shown in Table 2.1, along with the percentage of the entire sample each represented. They indicate that the survey methods were successful in obtaining an equal representation of males and females at each of the six age groups requested of Knowledge Networks.

A total of 623 males ages 18–93 years (49.9%) and 626 females ages 18–96 years completed the sample. However, just 10 participants were older than 87 years. The mean age for males was 49.7 years (SD = 18.0), and for females was 49.8 years (SD = 18.0); these were not significantly different (F = 0.003, p = NS). (Note that henceforth, statistical significance for the demographic factors is set at $p \leq .05$.) The U.S. Census for 2000 indicated that 49.1% of the U.S. population was male, and thus our sample's sex distribution approximated that of the United States generally. Nearly equal numbers of males and females were placed into four educational categories, so that the sexes did not differ in their educational levels (χ^2 = 0.60, p = NS), as shown in Table 2.2. The educational levels of the normative sample were also generally comparable to those of the U.S. population as reflected in the 2000 U.S. Census, although the normative sample contained a slightly lower

TABLE 2.1. The Numbers of Males and Females in Six Age Groups in the BFIS Normative Sample

Sex and age group	Frequency	Percent	Cumulative percent
Male 18–29	104	8.3	8.3
Male 30–39	102	8.2	16.5
Male 40–49	104	8.3	24.8
Male 50–59	104	8.3	33.1
Male 60–69	104	8.3	41.5
Male 70+	105	8.4	49.9
Female 18–29	102	8.2	58.0
Female 30–39	104	8.3	66.4
Female 40–49	105	8.4	74.8
Female 50–59	106	8.5	83.3
Female 60–69	105	8.4	91.7
Female 70+	104	8.3	100.0
Total	1,249	100.0	

TABLE 2.2. Education Levels for Each Sex in the Normative Sample, in Comparison to the 2000 U.S. Census

Education category		Sex: Male	Female	Total	Percent of U.S. Census[a]
Less than high school	Count	73	69	142	
	% within gender	11.7%	11.0%	11.4%	19.6%
High school	Count	178	190	368	
	% within gender	28.6%	30.4%	29.5%	28.6%
Some college	Count	182	183	365	
	% within gender	29.2%	29.2%	29.2%	21.0%
Bachelor's degree or higher	Count	190	184	374	
	% within gender	30.5%	29.4%	29.9%	24.1%

[a]Based on the 2000 U.S. Census (available at *www.census.gov*).

percentage of those with less than a high school education than was the case for the U.S. Census.

The geographic distribution of the participants within each sex is shown in Table 2.3. As this table indicates, males and females in the study were obtained from all four regions of the United States in relatively equal proportions. There was no significant difference in the geographic distributions as a function of participants' sex ($\chi^2 = 3.12$, p = NS). The results show that the geographic distribution of the normative sample was quite similar to that of the U.S. population, based on the 2000 U.S. Census.

TABLE 2.3. Regional Distribution by Sex for the Normative Sample, in Comparison to the 2000 U.S. Census

Region		Sex: Male	Female	Total	Percent of U.S. Census[a]
Northeast	Count	111	126	237	
	% within gender	17.8%	20.1%	19.0%	19.0%
Midwest	Count	133	150	283	
	% within gender	21.3%	24.0%	22.7%	22.9%
South	Count	237	219	456	
	% within gender	38.0%	35.0%	36.5%	35.6%
West	Count	142	131	273	
	% within gender	22.8%	20.9%	21.9%	22.4%

[a]Based on the 2000 U.S. Census (available at *www.census.gov*).

The racial/ethnic breakdown of the normative sample by sex is displayed in Table 2.4. As seen in that table, the majority of the participants were white (non-Hispanic), as was the case in the U.S. population. There were no significant differences in the ethnic breakdown of the sample for each sex (χ^2 = 2.34, p = NS). The percentage of participants for each ethnic group resembled to a large extent that for the U.S. population, based on the 2000 U.S. Census. However, blacks and Hispanics appeared to be slightly underrepresented in the normative sample.

The breakdown of the normative sample by income categories is shown in Table 2.5. The mean income category was 11.3, which translated into a mean income ranging from $40,000 to $49,999; the median category was 12, equivalent to an income ranging from $50,000 to $59,999. The modal income category was 13, reflecting a range of $60,000 to $69,999. The median household income of the United States was $41,994 as of the 2000 U.S. Census. The results suggest a relatively reasonable resemblance of the normative sample's household income to that of the U.S. population.

The marital status of the normative sample participants is shown in Table 2.6. It suggests a reasonable similarity between the normative sample and the U.S. population, based on the 2000 U.S. Census. However, a somewhat lower percentage of the normative sample appeared to have never been married than was the case in the U.S. Census. The U.S. Census Bureau computes marital status for persons 15 years of age and older, which would of course reflect a higher percentage having never been married than was the case for the normative sample, which included individuals 18 years of age and older. We would expect more of the latter group to be married, relative to the U.S. Census method of determining this figure. This probably

TABLE 2.4. Frequency and Percentage of Each Racial/Ethnic Group by Sex for the Normative Sample, in Comparison to the 2000 U.S. Census

		Sex			
Race/ethnic group		Male	Female	Total	Percent of U.S. Census[a]
White non-Hispanic	Count	478	488	966	
	% within gender	76.7%	78.0%	77.3%	75.1%
Black non-Hispanic	Count	43	42	85	
	% within gender	6.9%	6.7%	6.8%	12.3%
Other non-Hispanic	Count	20	27	47	
	% within gender	3.2%	4.3%	3.8%	6.6%
Hispanic	Count	61	50	111	
	% within gender	9.8%	8.0%	8.9%	12.5%
2+ races, non-Hispanic	Count	21	19	40	
	% within gender	3.4%	3.0%	3.2%	2.4%
Total		623	626	1,249	

[a]Based on the 2000 U.S. Census (available at *www.census.gov*).

TABLE 2.5. Distribution of Household Income Categories for the Normative Sample

Income category	Frequency	Percent	Cumulative percent
Less than $5,000	18	1.4	1.4
$5,000 to $7,499	21	1.7	3.1
$7,500 to $9,999	27	2.2	5.3
$10,000 to $12,499	36	2.9	8.2
$12,500 to $14,999	35	2.8	11.0
$15,000 to $19,999	55	4.4	15.4
$20,000 to $24,999	63	5.0	20.4
$25,000 to $29,999	70	5.6	26.0
$30,000 to $34,999	65	5.2	31.2
$35,000 to $39,999	79	6.3	37.6
$40,000 to $49,999	110	8.8	46.4
$50,000 to $59,999	116	9.3	55.6
$60,000 to $74,999	141	11.3	66.9
$75,000 to $84,999	89	7.1	74.1
$85,000 to $99,999	98	7.8	81.9
$100,000 to $124,999	99	7.9	89.8
$125,000 to $149,999	52	4.2	94.0
$150,000 to $174,999	36	2.9	96.9
$175,000 or more	39	3.1	100.0

TABLE 2.6. Marital Status of the Normative Sample, in Comparison to the 2000 U.S. Census

Marital status	Frequency	Percent	Percent of U.S. Census[a]
Married	659	52.8	54.4
Widowed	85	6.8	6.6
Divorced	118	9.4	9.7
Separated	28	2.2	2.2
Never married	264	21.1	27.1
Living with partner	95	7.6	—

[a]Based on the 2000 U.S. Census (available at *www.census.gov*).

TABLE 2.7. Employment Status of the Normative Sample

Employment status	Frequency	Percent	Cumulative percent
Working—as a paid employee	573	45.9	45.9
Working—self-employed	81	6.5	52.4
Not working—on temporary layoff from a job	20	1.6	54.0
Not working—looking for work	90	7.2	61.2
Not working—retired	282	22.6	83.7
Not working—disabled	99	7.9	91.7
Not working—other	104	8.3	100.0
Total	1,249	100.0	

explains the difference in marital status between the U.S. Census data and those for the normative sample.

The employment status of the normative sample is shown in Table 2.7. More than half of those in the sample were working as paid employees or in self-employment, and nearly a quarter of the respondents were in retirement. The 2000 U.S. Census figure for those currently employed was 57.5% for individuals 16 years of age and older. This indicates a reasonable similarity of the normative sample to the U.S. population in terms of employment status.

To summarize the demographic characteristics of the study sample, it appears that the normative sample recruited here closely approximated the U.S. adult population as reflected in the 2000 U.S. Census concerning regional distribution, sex, racial/ethnic group, marital status, employment status, total household income, and education. This was the normative sample on which data from the self-report versions of the BFIS were collected. The results for the factor analyses of the scale and construction of the individual subscales based on this normative sample's responses are discussed in the next chapter.

CHAPTER 3

Factor Analysis, Score Construction, and Item Frequencies

This chapter reports the results of the factor analyses intended to uncover the underlying dimensions of impairment on the BFIS. Next, the frequencies with which the items were endorsed by the normative sample are presented and discussed.

Factor Analysis

On average, participants in the normative sample answered 12 of the domains as being applicable to them ($M = 12.3$, $SD = 2.5$). Just 6% of the sample endorsed only 8 or fewer domains as applicable to them, while 90% answered that 10 or more of the domains applied to them and so chose to rate them; 65% rated at least 13 of the 15 domains. In short, most participants gave answers for the majority of the 15 BFIS domains.

The initial self-reports of the final 15 BFIS domains were submitted to a principal component factor analysis (PCFA), using the entire normative sample of 1,249 adults described in Chapter 2. Missing data (instances in which a domain was marked as "does not apply") were replaced with the mean. The initial results revealed a single factor that had an eigenvalue greater than 1. Because a single factor was obtained, no additional rotations were undertaken (varimax, promax, etc.). The results of the PCFA are shown in Table 3.1.[1]

[1]The BFIS items/domains are given in Tables 3.1 and 3.2, and in Table 4.1 in Chapter 4, precisely as they appear in the BFIS forms themselves (see the Appendix). For the sake of brevity and consistency, these shorter names for the domains are used hereafter in text and figures, as well as in later tables: (1) home–family; (2) home–chores; (3) work; (4) social–strangers; (5) social–friends; (6) community activities; (7) education; (8) marriage/cohabiting/dating; (9) money management; (10) driving; (11) sexual relations; (12) daily responsibilities; (13) self-care routines; (14) health maintenance; and (15) childrearing.

TABLE 3.1. Factor Loadings for BFIS Domains Based on PCFA

BFIS domain	Factor: 1
1. In your home life with your immediate family	.765
2. In getting chores completed at home and managing your household	.785
3. In your work or occupation	.714
4. In your social interactions with strangers and acquaintances	.750
5. In your relationships with friends	.824
6. In your activities in the community (church, clubs, social groups, organizations)	.750
7. In any educational activities (college, night classes, technical training, occupational training)	.622
8. In your marital, co-living, or dating relationships	.759
9. In your management of your money, your bills, and your debts	.710
10. In driving a motor vehicle and in your history of citations and accidents	.615
11. In your sexual activities and sex relations with others	.587
12. In your organization and management of your daily responsibilities	.842
13. In caring for yourself daily (dressing, bathing and hygiene, eating, sleeping, etc.)	.754
14. In maintaining your health (exercise, nutrition, preventive medical and dental care, etc.)	.749
15. In taking care of and raising your children	.619

The single factor (eigenvalue = 7.93) accounted for 52.9% of the variance, and all 15 domains had moderate to high loadings on this factor (at least .587 or higher). The factor could be called an Adaptive–Social Impairment factor because it received its highest loadings (≥.750) from these domains (in descending order): daily responsibilities (.842), social–friends (.824), home–chores (.785), home–family (.765), marriage/cohabiting/dating (.759), self-care routines (.754), social–strangers (.750), and community activities (.750).

The factor structure closely resembles that found for earlier rating methods of impairment discussed in Chapter 1, such as the LIFE-RIFT (Leon et al., 1999). That scale, intended for use in evaluating impairment from mental disorders, contains just four domains (work, interpersonal relations, recreation, and global satisfaction). Each domain is rated by the interviewer on a scale of 0 (not applicable) to 5 (severe impairment), with a 6 indicating that no information is available. The interview does not have norms. Factor analysis of this interview found a single factor, which remained stable at a second follow-up evaluation. This is also true for the PIRS as discussed in Chapter 1, which is an interviewer-completed scale focusing on employability (adaptation); concentration, persistence, and pace; social and recreational; travel; social function (relationships); and self-care and hygiene domains (Davies, 2008). Each domain is rated by the interviewer on a 5-point scale. Factor analysis reveals a single factor for this measure. Comparable domains of the BFIS also loaded on the large single Adaptive–Social Impairment factor. Likewise, a separate factor analysis of just the six domains used to create the BFIS Quick Screen (see below) again revealed just a single factor (eigenvalue = 3.58), accounting in this case for 59.6% of the variance.

These results are very similar to the results of a factor analysis of the 10 domains from the earlier prototype version of the BFIS, the IRS. The IRS was collected as part of the large UMASS Study of adults with ADHD, along with Clinical and Community control groups (Barkley et al., 2008). As noted in Chapter 2, the IRS assessed 10 domains, 9 of which were carried forward to the BFIS (only a rating on impairment in leisure activities was not included in the BFIS), with each domain rated 0–3. For the purpose of the present manual, a PCFA was conducted on the 10 domain scores of the IRS from that study, using the entire sample of participants. The results revealed a single factor (eigenvalue = 6.23), which accounted for 62.3% of the variance and contained all 10 domains, with factor loadings ranging from .421 (driving) to .727 (daily responsibilities).

The IRS was also used in the Milwaukee Study of hyperactive and control children followed to adulthood (Barkley et al., 2008). For the purposes of this manual, a PCFA was again conducted on the set of 10 domain ratings from this scale, using all participants in that study. The results were essentially the same as those for the UMASS Study: A single factor emerged (eigenvalue = 5.16), accounting for 51.6% of the variance and containing all 10 domain scores, with factor loadings ranging from .640 (driving) to .790 (social interactions). In general, it is clear that self-ratings of impairment—whether collected on the BFIS or IRS as self-ratings, or provided by clinicians on other measures, as done in earlier research—all appear to provide evidence for a single underlying factor of impairment across these measures.

Frequency of Domain Responses

It is clinically and scientifically informative to examine the percentage of respondents in the normative sample who endorsed each of the item answers. This gives an indication of how common or uncommon the different levels of impairment are for each domain (item). This information can also be used to determine what severity rating for each domain can be used to indicate that this domain at that rating can be judged to be functionally impaired—in other words, that such an answer or rating in that domain would be very atypical of the general population. For instance, if the vast majority of adults respond to a domain with not at all, somewhat, or mild (0–4 on the BFIS), then responses more severe than this (moderate, severe) could be considered to indicate likely impairment in that domain, relative to the average person. Of course, whether or not that domain is functionally impaired in reality is a question of validity. The clinician must evaluate that issue against other forms of information that would corroborate such a self-report, as discussed in Chapter 1. But it can still be of great clinical value to know just how often individuals describe themselves as having various degrees of difficulty with functioning in the 15 domains evaluated in the BFIS. To gain some idea about how often adults in a general population sample endorsed each possible answer for each domain, the percentage of adults in the normative sample who endorsed each of the possible answers to each domain was computed. The results appear in Table 3.2. This is important information for medical and mental health professionals, and for others who may have an interest in knowing the proportion of the population endorsing particular levels of functional difficulties (impairment) in these 15 domains of major life activities.

TABLE 3.2. Percentage of the Normative Sample Endorsing "Does Not Apply," Percentage of the Normative Sample to Whom a Domain Did Apply, and Who Endorsed Each Level of Impairment for Each Domain on the BFIS

		Degree of rated impairment (functional difficulties)[b]									
	Does not	None	Somewhat		Mild		Moderate			Severe	
BFIS domain	apply[a]	0	1	2	3	4	5	6	7	8	9
1. In your home life with your immediate family	13.5	33.3	24.8	12.6	7.2	6.3	6.6	4.7	3.1	0.9	0.6
2. In getting chores completed at home and managing your household	3.7	21.9	19.6	14.3	10.9	7.5	8.8	7.2	4.9	3.2	1.7
3. In your work or occupation	29.9	30.3	24.6	15.3	7.4	5.4	6.4	5.3	2.9	1.5	1.0
4. In your social interactions with strangers and acquaintances	4.0	25.5	25.0	14.8	7.6	7.9	8.1	4.3	3.4	1.8	1.5
5. In your relationships with friends	4.2	32.6	25.8	13.9	8.3	5.4	6.2	3.8	2.4	1.0	0.8
6. In your activities in the community (church, clubs, social groups, organizations)	25.9	30.9	24.3	14.3	10.3	3.9	7.0	3.6	3.0	1.1	1.6
7. In any educational activities (college, night classes, technical training, occupational training)	57.8	34.5	19.4	11.8	6.6	3.8	10.2	3.8	4.0	2.8	3.0
8. In your marital, co-living, or dating relationships	21.6	29.4	22.9	15.3	6.5	4.8	7.5	4.9	3.9	3.1	1.7
9. In your management of your money, your bills, and your debts	4.5	34.0	21.3	14.0	6.3	6.0	7.0	3.9	3.7	1.2	2.8
10. In driving a motor vehicle and in your history of citations and accidents	11.4	52.5	25.0	7.6	3.9	2.4	4.2	2.1	1.4	0.5	0.4
11. In your sexual activities and sex relations with others	23.3	32.5	18.0	12.4	9.4	4.6	6.9	5.0	4.7	2.9	3.7
12. In your organization and management of your daily responsibilities	4.2	29.2	23.9	15.1	7.9	5.7	6.9	4.8	3.6	1.6	1.3
13. In caring for yourself daily (dressing, bathing and hygiene, eating, sleeping, etc.)	3.0	50.9	21.3	9.0	3.7	2.2	4.6	3.4	2.6	1.2	1.0
14. In maintaining your health (exercise, nutrition, preventive medical and dental care, etc.)	3.2	29.1	19.7	14.6	10.0	6.3	7.3	5.8	3.4	1.4	2.4
15. In taking care of and raising your children	58.6	41.4	21.1	13.7	6.0	2.9	6.6	3.5	2.3	1.4	1.2

[a]Percentages in this column reflect the percentage of the entire normative sample specifying that this domain did not apply to them.
[b]Percentages in the remaining columns (marked 0–9) are the percentages of people who did believe that this domain applied to them, and so chose to rate their degree of impairment.

This table clearly shows the extent of the non-normality of the distributions for these 15 domains. The distributions of the answers are highly skewed to the left (or toward low ratings), as expected for a scale that focuses on impairment in a general population. Such a result has been observed for other rating scales of impairment, in research using much smaller samples (see Davies, 2008). This explains why raw scores have not been converted to *T*-scores to smooth out and partially normalize these distributions in creating the score sheets for the BFIS. Such a practice would artificially warp the percentiles that would be determined from such a conversion, so that they would not be those actually obtained in the normative sample. Instead, the score sheets indicate the actual percentile in the normative sample associated with each score.

Table 3.2 also clearly shows that for the vast majority of domains, the vast majority of the normative sample endorsed most items at a severity of not at all, somewhat, or mild. Answers reflecting moderate or severe impairment (5–7 or 8–9, respectively) are statistically unusual (and even rare, in the case of 8–9). The latter ratings were endorsed by less than 2% of the normative population. Less than 6–10% in most cases gave answers of 5–7. How much difficulty (how high a rating) must an individual report to be considered statistically unusual or abnormal? Most rating scales consider the 93rd–95th percentile (i.e., from 1 in 14 to 1 in 20 people in our normative sample) as probably indicative of being statistically deviant in a population. So if one wants to identify a domain as being impaired to a degree that is statistically rare (top 5th–7th percentile), then each domain can be examined for the score that signifies this threshold (93rd–95th percentile or higher). Here are the thresholds that were used to signify abnormality for the various domains in the BFIS:

- A score of 5 or higher would reach this threshold for two domains: home–family and driving.
- A score of 6 would reach this threshold for nine domains: work, social–strangers, social–friends, community activities, money management, daily responsibilities, self-care routines, health maintenance, and childrearing.
- A rating of 7 or higher would surpass this threshold for the four remaining domains: home–chores, education, marriage/cohabiting/dating, and sexual relations.

These thresholds are indicated on the score sheets in the Appendix in enlarged **boldface** type, in order to signify them (and higher scores) as the thresholds used here to determine functional impairment in each domain, relative to the average person. From this information, a clinician can now compute a score for the percentage of domains in which the individual placed in the impaired range, or a Percent Domains Impaired score.

Overall, 64% of participants had no scores that fell at or above these thresholds for abnormality (impairment). Another 12% reported 1 of the 15 domains as being impaired, another 7% reported 2 domains, and 4% reported 3 domains. Just 10% had scores on 5 or more domains that were impaired. And just 6% were impaired in 7 or more of the 15 domains. The mean number of domains falling in the impaired range was 1.3 (*SD* = 2.5).

But such figures are deceptive because not everyone answered every domain as being applicable to him/her. A better indicator here of the extensiveness or pervasiveness of impairment across domains is the percentage of domains rated by the respondents (domains that applied to them) in which the ratings placed in the abnormal or impaired range. In the normative sample, 63% of respondents were not impaired in any domain they rated (0% of domains rated were impaired). The mean percentage of domains impaired was 11% (*SD* = 20%). The mean is not the best index of central tendency in this distribution, however, because the distribution is so skewed toward the low range of percentages. For instance, 75% of the respondents reported impairment in 13% or fewer of the domains they rated, and 84% of participants reported impaired in just 25% or fewer of the domains they answered. Any participant whose ratings fell in the impairment zone in at least one-third (33%) of the domains they rated would be at the 89th percentile of the normative population. This is to say that just 10% of the normative sample was in the impaired range on one-third or more of the domains they rated. And anyone reporting half of all rated domains as being impaired would be at the 94th percentile of the population. In other words, a person completing the scale whose ratings are high enough to place in the impaired ranges on one-third to one-half or more of the domains the person has rated should be viewed as reporting a highly abnormal pervasiveness (number of different domains) of impairment.

Besides the score (rating) given on each of the 15 domains, a separate Mean Impairment Score can be computed for the scale. To do so, the scores for the domains in which a person has rated him-/herself (as opposed to indicating that it does not apply to him/her) are summed. This sum is then divided by the number of domains that do apply to this person (the number of domains that have contributed a score to the summation). To summarize, the BFIS long form (hereafter referred to as the BFIS-LF) can be used to obtain 17 scores: 15 individual domain ratings, a Mean Impairment Score, and a Percent Domains Impaired score.

Creating the BFIS Quick Screen

There may be instances in which the examiner wishes to conduct a very preliminary quick screening of an individual for the likelihood of functional impairment in those domains viewed by government agencies as important to the determination of a disability. On the BFIS, these domains are typically home–family, home–chores, self-care routines, social–friends, education, and work. Hence these six domains make up the BFIS Quick Screen. Separate scores can be obtained for each domain, along with a Mean Impairment Score and a Percent Domains Impaired score. The former score, again, is determined by summing the scores for all domains applicable to an individual and dividing this by the number of domains the individual has rated. The Percent Domains Impaired score is computed just as it is with the BFIS-LF: The clinician counts the number of domains that were rated in the impaired range, and divides this by the total number of domains that were rated. As noted above, these six domains form a single factor when submitted to factor analysis.

The results for the six individual domain ratings used to create the BFIS Quick Screen are also graphically depicted in Figure 3.1. This figure obviously illustrates

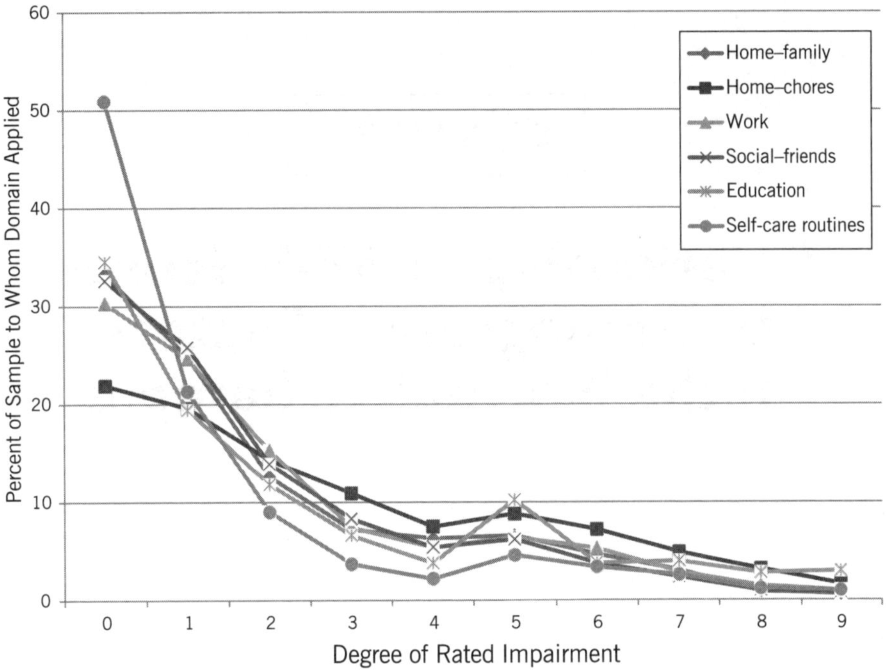

FIGURE 3.1. The percentage of the sample (to whom each domain applied) reporting each degree of impairment for each of the six domains constituting the BFIS Quick Screen. Domain names are as given in footnote 1 to chapter text.

the point made earlier about the marked skew in the distributions of these answers. It also again indicates that scores of moderate or higher severity were endorsed by only a minority of respondents in the normative sample. Again, this is why clinicians should consider such ratings to be statistically abnormal.

Summary

The BFIS-LF can be scored to yield (1) up to 15 different raw scores that can be converted to their associated percentiles, one for each domain; (2) a Mean Impairment Score, reflecting the sum of all rated domains (domains applicable to this person) divided by the number of domains the person has rated; and (3) a Percent Domains Impaired Score, reflecting the percentage of domains the person has rated that fall in the impaired range. The BFIS Quick Screen is scored to yield essentially the same three types of scores, but is only based on 6 of the 15 domains: (1) up to 6 domain scores and their respective percentiles, (2) a Mean Impairment Score, and (3) a Percent Domains Impaired score.

CHAPTER 4

Relationship of BFIS Scores to Demographic Factors in the Normative Sample

This chapter describes the relationship of various demographic factors to the BFIS scores for the entire normative sample of 1,249 adults. This was done to determine the best means of presenting the normative data (percentiles) on the score sheets in the Appendix. Yet it also sheds light on the relationship of these demographic factors (age, sex, ethnicity, geographic region) to self-reported levels of impairment in a general population sample.

Age

Age was found to correlate to a low but significant and negative degree with 14 of the 15 domain scores, with significant Pearson correlations ranging from –.09 (childrearing) to –.22 (money management) (all p's $< .05$). The exception was the domain of sexual relations (.01), which was not significantly related to age. As a consequence, both the Mean Impairment Score for the BFIS-LF ($r = -.17$, $n = 1{,}232$, $p < .001$) and that for the 6-item BFIS Quick Screen ($r = -.15$, $n = 1{,}231$, $p < .001$) were also significantly correlated with age, as were the Percent Domains Impaired score for the BFIS-LF ($r = -.15$, $n = 1{,}232$, $p < .001$), and for the BFIS Quick Screen ($r = -.11$, $n = 1{,}231$, $p < .001$). In general, specific ratings of impairment in the domains on the BFIS shared less than 5% of their variance with age, and this relationship was less than 3% for both Mean Impairment Scores and both Percent Domains Impaired scores. The small negative relationship suggests that impairment ratings may decline slightly with age.

However, correlation analyses can disguise nonlinear effects within such data, particularly when there is good reason to believe that a nonlinear relationship might exist between impairment ratings and age. For instance, impairment may be elevated in young people, may decline with age to mid- to late life, but then may increase in old age. The relationship of age to the impairment scores was therefore also examined by using the seven age groupings (18–29, 30–39, 40–49, 50–59, 60–69, 70–79, and 80+ years) in the normative sample in a one-way (age group) analysis of variance. The effect of age was significant (all p's $< .05$) for 13 of the 15 BFIS domains, and for the Mean Impairment Scores and the Percent Domain Impaired scores from both the BFIS-LF and the BFIS Quick Screen. The two exceptions were the domains of sexual relations and childrearing. Mean differences across the age groups were minor and typically averaged just 0.5–1 point. The results for the Mean Impairment Scores for each of these initial seven age groups for both the BFIS-LF and the BFIS Quick Screen are shown in Figure 4.1. The patterns seen in this figure essentially duplicate those evident on each of the 15 individual domain ratings.

Pairwise comparisons of the age groups indicated that no contrasts were significant for the domains of work, education, sexual relations, self-care routines, and childrearing. Thus, despite the significant omnibus effect for work, education, and self-care routines, individual age group pairwise comparisons were not significant. Across the remaining domains, comparisons indicated that 18- to 29-year-olds were typically rated as more impaired than those in the 60- to 80+-year age groups on most domains, with the other age groups (30–59) falling between these two groupings. If the younger age groups differed from any group, it was from the 60- to 80+-year-old age groups in most cases. This was also the case for the two Percent Domains Impaired scores. Again, pairwise contrasts show that the age groups between 18 and 59 years reported just 11–13% of domains they rated as falling in the impaired range (see Chapter 3 for thresholds defining impaired or abnormal

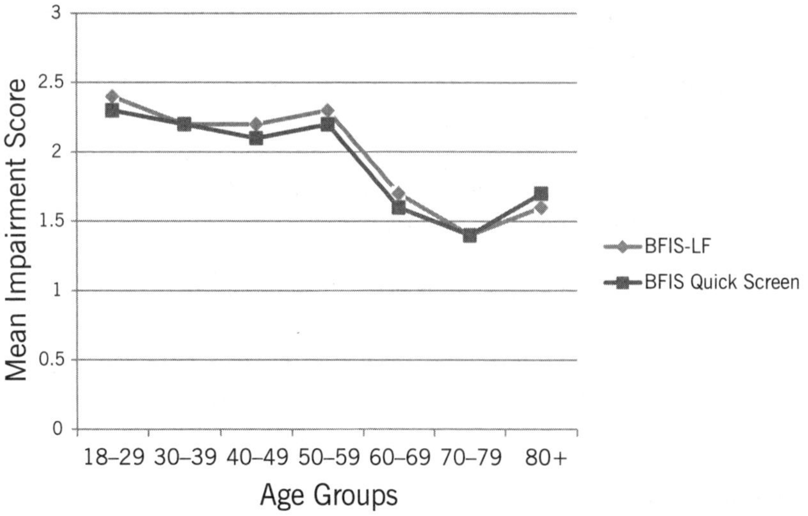

FIGURE 4.1. Mean Impairment Scores for the BFIS-LF and BFIS Quick Screen for each of seven age groups: 18–29, 30–39, 40–49, 50–59, 60–69, 70–79, and 80+ years.

scores on each domain) and did not differ from each other in these respects. Individuals 60 and older reported an even lower percentage (just 5–7%) of the domains they rated as being impaired. These older age groups (60–69, 70–79, and 80+) did not differ among themselves, but did differ from the 18- to 59-year-olds in these percent scores.

The slight decline in Mean Impairment Scores with age reflected in the correlations reported earlier is actually more of a step-like relationship. People between 18 and 59 years of age reported higher levels of mean impairment and a somewhat greater percentage of impaired domains than did individuals from 60 to 79 years of age. There appeared to be a slight uptick in impairment ratings at age 80 and older, but these were not significantly different from those in the 60–69 and 70–79 age groups.

This step-like decline in Mean Impairment Scores at age 60 could reflect a true developmental decline in current impairment with advancing age, at least to 80+ years. This decline, particularly after age 60, could be the result of both retiring from the workforce and having offspring leave home to become independent. Both of these events would have a significant impact on these and related domains (money management, marriage/cohabiting/dating, home–chores, etc.). Or the decline could reflect a cohort effect, in which older individuals recruited into studies such as this either have less impairment or at least report less impairment than younger adults so recruited. In other words, the older people become and the more impaired they become, the less likely they may be to participate in such survey research, for some unknown reason.

A third explanation is that the decline could be evidence for a differential survival rate, in which individuals with initially higher levels of impairment have shorter life expectancies and so are being culled from the population with advancing age. This idea has some merit. There is substantial evidence concerning the greater risk such impaired people may have for life-threatening events (e.g., accidental injuries, car accidents, work-related accidents), as well as for health-related lifestyle factors (greater smoking, greater use of alcohol and drugs, poorer dental health, greater body mass indices with age, etc.). There is the added factor here that greater impairment is also associated with greater stress, which itself may generate an increased likelihood of diseases and disorders that have the potential to shorten one's life. Also, impairment could easily be related to the personality trait of conscientiousness, such that lower levels of conscientiousness lead to higher impairment scores. Research has shown that individuals placing in the lower quartile of conscientiousness have a shorter life expectancy by an average of 7 years than do those with higher levels of this trait (Friedman et al., 1995). Of course, it is also possible that all of the explanations suggested above are operative in such a cross-sectional design as this one in studying age-related changes in impairment ratings.

Inspection of all the results for age, along with the distributions for the scores on each scale, indicated that three large age groupings could be created from the initial seven discussed above. It made sense to keep the 18- to 39-year-olds as a separate group from the 60- to 80+-year-olds, as most of the significant differences that occurred were found between these two groupings. Although the 40- to 59-year-olds did not differ significantly from the younger age group, they were made into a single and separate age grouping here, in order to create approximately equal sample sizes of middle-aged, young, and old participants. The 60+-year-olds would then serve as the final age group, given that on no comparisons were the age groups in the 60–80+ range found to differ from each other. Only seven participants were 90 years of age and older; given that this older age group was not well represented in the normative sample, they were excluded from further consideration. Thus the normative information for the BFIS score sheets in the Appendix is based on individuals between 18 and 89 years of age. The final three age groupings were 18–39, 40–59, and 60–89 years. These yielded sample sizes of 412, 419, and 411, respectively, for a total sample of 1,242.

The results for all of the BFIS scores and the statistical comparisons among these three age groups are shown in Table 4.1. Even when these three larger age groupings were created as described above, it was still evident that significant effects of age existed for nearly all domain scores except sexual relations and childrearing, where no effect of age was significant. With two exceptions, pairwise comparisons among the three age groups routinely found that the 60- to 89-year-olds gave lower impairment ratings than those in the two younger age groups. However, for the domain of education, the 18–39 group reported significantly higher impairment ratings than either of the two remaining age groups. This result was not terribly surprising, since younger adults are typically more involved in the education domain than are those in midlife or older. This finding made it clear that the norms (percentiles) for the BFIS scores would need to be presented specifically for each of these three age groups on the score sheets. Even so, the mean score differences (declines) across the age groupings were quite small and would have little clinical significance, except perhaps at extreme ends of these distributions.

Sex

A comparison of the 621 males with the 621 females from the revised (reduced) sample of 18- to 89-year-olds ($N = 1,242$) was conducted via a two-factor (age group × sex) analysis of variance applied to each score. The results indicated no significant main effects of sex on any of the 15 domain scores. None of the comparisons on the Mean Impairment Scores for either the BFIS-LF or the BFIS Quick Screen were significant, nor were the comparisons on the Percent Domains Impaired Scores from either form. In none of these analyses was there any significant interaction of age with sex. Because there were no sex differences, the normative data for the BFIS are not broken down by sex on the score sheets in the Appendix.

Ethnic Group

The next issue to address in considering how best to present the norms for scoring purposes was whether there existed any significant relationship of ethnic group to the BFIS scores. Before ethnic group comparisons were conducted, the groups were compared on their ages. Given that age effects were evident (see above) on most scores, if the groups should differ in their ages, age would need to serve as a covariate in such analyses. One-way analysis of variance revealed significant age differ-

TABLE 4.1. Results for the BFIS Domain Scores, Mean Impairment Scores, and Percent Domain Impaired Scores for Each of Three Age Groupings in the Normative Sample

	Age groups								
	1. 18–39		2. 40–59		3. 60–89				
Score	Mean	*SD*	Mean	*SD*	Mean	*SD*	*F*	*p*	Contrasts
1. In your home life with your immediate family	2.1	2.3	2.0	2.1	1.6	1.9	6.45	.002	1,2 > 3
2. In getting chores completed at home and managing your household	3.0	2.6	3.0	2.5	2.2	2.2	14.60	<.001	1,2 > 3
3. In your work or occupation	2.3	2.3	2.0	2.3	1.7	1.8	3.87	.021	1,2 > 3
4. In your social interactions with strangers and acquaintances	2.4	2.3	1.8	2.0	2.3	2.3	14.45	<.001	1,2 > 3
5. In your relationships with friends	2.1	2.3	2.0	2.1	1.4	1.7	13.61	<.001	1,2 > 3
6. In your activities in the community (church, clubs, social groups, organizations)	2.2	2.3	2.2	2.3	1.6	2.0	7.59	.001	1,2 > 3
7. In any educational activities (college, night classes, technical training, occupational training)	2.7	2.8	2.0	2.4	1.8	2.2	5.93	.003	1 > 2,3
8. In your marital, co-living, or dating relationships	2.7	2.6	2.4	2.5	1.6	2.0	18.39	<.001	1,2 > 3
9. In your management of your money, your bills, and your debts	2.6	2.7	2.3	2.4	1.4	1.9	31.22	<.001	1,2 > 3
10. In driving a motor vehicle and in your history of citations and accidents	1.4	2.1	1.2	1.8	0.8	1.3	8.51	<.001	1,2 > 3
11. In your sexual activities and sex relations with others	2.3	2.6	2.6	2.7	2.3	2.6	1.66	NS	
12. In your organization and management of your daily responsibilities	2.5	2.5	2.3	2.4	1.6	1.8	17.42	<.001	1,2 > 3
13. In caring for yourself daily (dressing, bathing and hygiene, eating, sleeping, etc.)	1.6	2.4	1.5	2.2	1.0	1.7	9.54	<.001	1,2 > 3
14. In maintaining your health (exercise, nutrition, preventive medical and dental care, etc.)	2.7	2.6	2.7	2.5	1.6	2.0	26.02	<.001	1,2 > 3
15. In taking care of and raising your children	1.9	2.4	1.6	1.9	1.4	2.1	2.55	NS	

(cont.)

TABLE 4.1. *(cont.)*

	Age groups								
	1. 18–39		2. 40–59		3. 60–89				
Score	Mean	*SD*	Mean	*SD*	Mean	*SD*	*F*	*p*	Contrasts
Mean Impairment Score—BFIS-LF	2.3	1.9	2.2	1.8	1.6	1.5	22.26	<.001	1,2 > 3
Percent Domains Impaired—BFIS-LF	13.5	22.6	12.3	21.1	6.4	15.9	14.58	<.001	1,2 > 3
Mean Impairment Score—BFIS Quick Screen	2.3	2.0	2.2	1.9	1.6	1.6	17.90	<.001	1,2 > 3
Percent Domains Impaired—BFIS Quick Screen	13.1	24.9	12.1	23.4	6.3	17.7	10.86	<.001	1,2 > 3

Note. F, results for the *F*-test from the analysis of variance; *p*, probability value for the *F*-test if ≤.05; NS,not significant. Contrasts are the results of the pairwise comparisons of the three age groups where $p \leq .05$.

ences among the five ethnic groups ($F = 5.89$, $p < .001$). Pairwise comparisons of the groups indicated that the white sample (*M* = 50.7, *SD* = 17.6) was significantly older than the Hispanic sample (*M* = 42.7, *SD* = 17.5). Otherwise, these groups did not differ from any of the others (black, other non-Hispanic, 2+ races non-Hispanic). This meant that age would need to serve as a covariate in the ethnic group comparisons of the BFIS scores.

There was no significant main effect for ethnic group on 14 of the 15 BFIS-LF domain ratings. However, significant effects were evident for driving ($F = 6.78$, $p < .001$). Pairwise contrasts on the driving ratings indicated that blacks reported higher impairment ratings (*M* = 2.2, *SD* = 2.6) than all other ethnic groups (white *M* = 1.03, *SD* = 1.7; Hispanic *M* = 1.5, *SD* = 2.2; other non-Hispanic [predominantly Asian] *M* = 1.1, *SD* = 1.4; and multiracial *M* = 0.8, *SD* = 1.2). Also, Hispanics reported more driving difficulties than did whites. No other pairwise comparisons were significant.

There was no main effect for ethnicity on the Mean Impairment Score for the BFIS-LF, but there was such an effect on the BFIS-LF Percent Domains Impaired score ($F = 4.47$, $p = .001$). Pairwise comparisons indicated that whites (*M* = 9.3%, *SD* = 18.6%) had a lower Percent Domain Impaired score than did either blacks (*M* = 16.6%, *SD* = 25.2%) or Hispanics (*M* = 16.8%, *SD* = 25.8%), who did not differ from each other or from those of other non-Hispanic ethnicity (*M* = 12.5%, *SD* = 20.6%) or multiracial classification (*M* = 14.0%, *SD* = 23.7%). On the BFIS Quick Screen, there was no main effect for ethnicity on the Mean Impairment Score, duplicating what was found on the BFIS-LF for this same score. But, once more, the Percent Domains Impaired score for the BFIS Quick Screen showed a main effect for ethnic group. The pattern of the pairwise comparisons was identical to that just described for this same score from the BFIS-LF. The differences between means in these few comparisons on which main effects for ethnic differences emerged were clinically trivial, however (an average of 0.5- to 1.0-point differences on a rating that spans 10 points). They probably achieved statistical significance because of the large sample sizes. Finally, no ethnic differences were evident on the other 14 specific domain scores or on the Mean Impairment Scores. For these reasons, the norms for the BFIS are not presented with any breakdown for ethnic groups in the Appendix.

Geographic Region

Finally, it seemed important to determine whether there existed any geographic regional differences in the BFIS scores that might have importance for the interpretation of the norms. An analysis of variance was conducted to compare results for the four major regions of the United States, using the entire normative sample ($N = 1,249$). There were no significant differences for 14 of the 15 domain ratings in the long-form version, or for the Mean Impairment Scores or the Percent Domains Impaired scores for either version of the scale. The one geographic difference that did reach significance was in the domain of self-care routines ($F = 2.88$, $p = .035$), with participants in the South ($M = 1.5$, $SD = 2.3$) and West ($M = 1.5$, $SD = 2.1$) reporting slightly greater difficulties than those in the Northeast ($M = 1.2$, $SD = 1.9$) or Midwest ($M = 1.2$, $SD = 1.9$). No other comparisons were significant. Again, the differences were trivial, even if statistically significant, and were not evident on any other scores. The possible reasons for this difference are not obvious. The normative information is therefore not displayed with any breakdown by U.S. regions in the score sheets in the Appendix.

Creation of the BFIS-LF and BFIS Quick Screen Score Sheets

BFIS-LF Score Sheets

Two versions (Self- and Other-Report) of the BFIS-LF are provided in the Appendix. Norms are provided for just the Self-Report version, however. There are no norms for the Other-Report form, which is used only to collect corroborative information on impairment from someone who knows a participant well. One score sheet was created for *each* of the three age groups. The norms presented on each sheet are set forth separately for each of the 15 specific domains, for the Mean Impairment Score, and for the Percent Domains Impaired score.

The means and standard deviations for each domain for each of these three age groupings are shown in Table 4.1 and discussed above. These distributions were used to create the score sheets in the Appendix. The percentile scores for each age group are shown in that group's respective score sheet. Raw score ranges for each domain score are presented starting with the 1st–50th percentiles and then for the 50th–75th and 76th–84th percentiles because scores in these ranges are normal and not of clinical interest (other than to signify that a rating was in the normal range). Percentile equivalents for each individual score from that point onward are provided separately for the 85th through 99th percentiles. This was done because it is only near the extreme upper ends of the distributions that the percentiles become truly useful for clinical purposes—that is, identifying individuals with age-inappropriate impairment ratings.

BFIS Quick Screen Score Sheets

The Appendix also includes Self- and Other-Report versions of the BFIS Quick Screen. Both versions contain those six domains believed to be the most important in making impairment and disability determinations during clinical evaluations. A separate BFIS Quick Screen score sheet was created for the Self-Report version only; this sheet includes a section for each of the three age groupings. Each section gives raw scores and their percentile equivalents, portrayed in the same way as in the BFIS-LF score sheets (see above). Norms are also provided for the Mean Impairment Score and the Percent Domains Impaired score.

BFIS Impairment Interview

A separate BFIS Impairment Interview is provided for use as a follow-up to the completion of the rating scales, although no norms were collected on the interview form. Clinicians are strongly encouraged to use this interview to gather more specific information about the basis for any self-ratings in any domains that were in the moderate (5–7) or higher range. Such ratings would be at the 93rd–95th percentile or higher for 13 of the 15 major life domains on the BFIS-LF. The interview gives a clinician an opportunity to determine the veracity or legitimacy of an individual's self-report of such high impairment by asking for specific details that led this participant to rate any domains this high or higher. The Impairment Interview form contains all 15 domains from the BFIS-LF. The clinician does not need to interview the participant about all domains—just those on which the ratings were sufficiently high to be abnormal or unusual relative to the general population. The interview is not scored, but the form in the Appendix serves as a recording device for this important follow-up interview. On the basis of the participant's detailed explanations of any impaired domains, the clinician may elect to obtain official archival records for that domain (if any are available) to corroborate these self-reports of impairment. Obtaining the reports of someone else who knows the index person well is also strongly encouraged. This provides further information to corroborate the index person's reports. And it gives the clinician a means of triangulating all sources of information, so as to make an informed judgment about the extent and pervasiveness of the individual's impairments (see Chapter 1).

CHAPTER 5

Reliability

This brief chapter presents the information that is available concerning the various forms of reliability for the BFIS. More research on these and other psychometric characteristics of the scale is welcome. What information is available indicates that the reliability of the scale is quite satisfactory for use of the scale in clinical, research, and industrial/organizational settings where the assessment of psychosocial impairment is of interest.

Internal Consistency

The internal consistency of the BFIS-LF domain ratings (Cronbach's alpha) was found to be quite satisfactory (alpha = .969, $F = 32.60$, $p < .001$). This is not surprising, given the relatively high factor loadings of each of the 15 domains on the single factor found in the factor analysis reported in Chapter 3. All of this suggests that higher impairment ratings in any one domain are also related to a strong tendency for higher ratings to be found in other domains. The internal consistency of the BFIS Quick Screen was nearly as high (alpha = .916, $F = 11.90$, $p < .001$). This is also evident below in the correlations among the domain ratings.

Test–Retest Reliability

As noted in Chapter 2, test–retest reliability was assessed by having a subset of 62 adults complete the BFIS on a second occasion 2–3 weeks after initially completing the scale. Half of the participants at each age level were men, and half were women. At least 10 from each of the original six age groups participated. Missing data (refused responses) occurred on only a few items and were limited to only one to three (1.6–4.8%) missing responses. In most of those instances, just one missing response per domain occurred. As with the initial dataset, these missing responses were replaced by a 99 (does not apply). The Pearson product–moment correlations between the first and second administrations were as follows: home–family ($r = .52$); home–chores (.52); work (.66); social–strangers (.72); social–friends (.71); community activities (.50); education (.40); marriage/cohabiting/dating (.68); money management (.47); driving (.71); sexual relations (.46); daily responsibilities (.54); self-care routines (.49); health maintenance (.41); and childrearing (.60) (all p's < .001) . The test–retest reliability for the Mean Impairment Score on the BFIS-LF was .72 ($p < .001$), and for the Percent Domains Impaired score it was .53 ($p < .001$). For the BFIS Quick Screen, the test–retest reliability for the Mean Impairment Score was similar to that for the BFIS-LF, being .71 ($p < .001$); the reliability for the Percent Domains Impaired score was likewise similar to that for the BFIS-LF, being .53 ($p < .001$). These results show moderate to high reliability across this time period, with the most satisfactory reliabilities occurring for the specific domain scores of social–strangers, social–friends, driving, work, marriage/cohabiting/dating, and childrearing. Clearly, though, the most reliable score to use may be the Mean Impairment Score from either form, rather than the individual domain ratings.

Another means of examining the issue of test–retest stability of the BFIS domain scores is to compare the actual scores from the initial testing and retesting administrations. This was done by using a paired-samples *t*-test. The results are shown in Table 5.1. They indicate that for the vast majority of domain scores, the first and second administrations did not yield significantly different results. But three domain scores did decline significantly from pre- to posttesting: those for social–strangers, social–friends, and marriage/cohabiting/dating. Though statistically significant, the declines in the individual domain impairment ratings were slight. As for the summary scores, the Mean Impairment Score for the BFIS-LF showed a slight but significant decline from pre- to posttesting, but the changes in the Percent Domains Impaired score for this form did not change across time. For the BFIS Quick Screen, neither the Mean Impairment Score nor the Percent Domains Impaired score changed significantly from pre- to posttesting. These results suggest satisfactory stability for the vast majority of BFIS scores over this period of assessment.

Relationships among Domain Scores

As indicated by the factor analysis reported earlier, self-ratings of current degree of impairment appeared to constitute a single large underlying dimension. It is therefore not surprising to find that the individual BFIS domain scores were likewise intercorrelated. The relationships among the domain scores were evaluated by using Pearson product–moment correlations based on the entire sample of 1,249 participants. The results appear in Table 5.2. They demonstrate that the scores were significantly and moderately intercorrelated, with relationships ranging from .34 to .77, so that the domain ratings shared anywhere from 11.5% to 59.2% of their variance. The pattern of relationships is quite sensible, with stronger relation-

TABLE 5.1. Comparison of Initial and Retesting Sample Results on BFIS Domain Ratings, Mean Impairment, and Percent Domains Impaired Scores ($n = 62$)

	Initial		Retesting				
Score	Mean	*SD*	Mean	*SD*	Mean diff.	*t*	*p*
Home–family	1.37	2.14	1.37	2.10	0.00	0.00	NS
Home–chores	2.19	2.33	2.48	2.65	–0.29	–0.92	NS
Work	0.98	2.39	0.77	2.08	0.21	0.88	NS
Social–strangers	2.16	2.52	1.63	1.98	0.53	2.38	.021
Social–friends	1.85	2.27	1.23	1.75	0.63	3.07	.003
Community activities	1.21	2.20	0.71	1.69	0.50	1.97	NS
Education	0.39	2.15	0.02	2.01	0.37	1.27	NS
Marriage/cohabiting/dating	1.64	2.66	1.05	2.04	0.60	2.38	.020
Money management	1.66	2.21	1.68	2.13	–0.02	–0.06	NS
Driving	0.95	1.88	1.00	1.97	–0.05	–0.26	NS
Sexual relations	1.32	2.69	1.08	2.42	0.24	0.72	NS
Daily responsibilities	1.71	2.10	1.34	1.84	0.37	1.53	NS
Self-care routines	0.84	1.55	0.89	1.60	–0.48	–0.24	NS
Health maintenance	1.61	2.22	1.60	2.13	0.02	0.05	NS
Childrearing	1.16	2.07	0.77	1.70	0.39	1.78	NS
Mean Impairment Score—BFIS-LF	1.85	1.75	1.49	1.62	0.36	2.25	.028
Percent Domains Impaired—BFIS-LF	9.07	17.02	5.98	16.67	3.09	1.46	NS
Mean Impairment Score—BFIS Quick Screen	1.74	1.69	1.49	1.70	0.24	1.48	NS
Percent Domains Impaired—BFIS Quick Screen	7.89	16.35	6.92	19.44	0.97	0.43	NS

Note. Mean diff., differences in the initial and retesting means; *t*, results for the paired-samples *t*-test; *p*, probability value for the *t*-test if $\leq .05$; NS, not significant.

ships being evident for overlapping domains, and weaker ones being evident where domains are not as conceptually or practically related to each other. For instance, it makes sense that an impairment rating in the home–family domain would be more closely related to those in marriage/cohabiting/dating, home–chores, daily responsibilities, and childrearing than to those in work, community activities, driving, or social–strangers.

Interobserver Agreement and Disparity

The extent to which self-ratings on any psychological ability or behavioral performance agree with those provided by others about the examinees is evidence of both

TABLE 5.2. Intercorrelations among the BFIS Domain Scores (Self-Ratings)

Domains	1	2	3	4	5	6	7	8	9	10	11	12	13	14	15
1. Home–family	—														
2. Home–chores	.65	—													
3. Work	.67	.64	—												
4. Social–strangers	.58	.54	.64	—											
5. Social–friends	.68	.58	.68	.77	—										
6. Community activities	.63	.62	.64	.73	.77	—									
7. Education	.61	.61	.68	.66	.66	.73	—								
8. Marriage/cohabitation/dating	.74	.66	.64	.60	.70	.67	.68	—							
9. Money management	.56	.59	.54	.48	.55	.58	.58	.59	—						
10. Driving	.52	.40	.51	.44	.53	.54	.55	.49	.47	—					
11. Sexual relations	.48	.50	.46	.44	.52	.54	.49	.60	.40	.34	—				
12. Daily responsibilities	.65	.75	.71	.59	.65	.68	.77	.65	.64	.48	.54	—			
13. Self-care routines	.57	.60	.57	.48	.59	.61	.58	.55	.51	.46	.48	.70	—		
14. Health maintenance	.53	.64	.53	.51	.55	.60	.60	.57	.57	.40	.50	.68	.70	—	
15. Childrearing	.75	.60	.65	.60	.70	.70	.67	.68	.56	.66	.52	.66	.77	.59	—

Note. All correlations are statistically significant at $p < .001$.

reliability and (more likely) validity. The BFIS was not administered to significant others who knew the participants in the normative study well, so we could not evaluate the correspondence between these self-ratings and those provided by informed others or collaterals. But such evidence was available from several previous studies using the prototype of the BFIS, the IRS. This research can speak to the extent to which self- and other-ratings of impairment are likely to agree.

One of these studies, the UMASS Study, was a large project evaluating the nature of symptoms, impairments, and deficits in executive functioning in three groups of participants ages 18–60 years (see Barkley et al., 2008; Barkley & Murphy, 2010, in press): (1) 146 adults clinically diagnosed with ADHD; (2) a Clinical control group of 97 adults evaluated at the same clinic but not diagnosed with ADHD; and (3) a Community control group of 109 adult volunteers from the local community. Both the adults with ADHD and the Clinical control adults were obtained from consecutive referrals to an adult ADHD clinic in a department of psychiatry at a regional medical school. The Community adults were obtained from advertisements posted throughout the medical school and from periodic newspaper ads in the regional newspaper. More information on these samples can be found in the Barkley and colleagues (2008) book. Slightly more than two-thirds (68%) of our group with ADHD were male, which differed from a nearly equal sex distribution (51%) in our Community control group, but was not significantly different from that evident in the Clinical control group (56%). The vast majority of participants were white (94%) or of European American ancestry, and the groups did not differ in this respect. Therefore, caution is warranted in extrapolating the initial results reported below to adults in other ethnic groups.

We had participation from others on 129 members (88%) of the ADHD group, 88 members (90%) of the Clinical group, and 92 members (84%) of the Community group. These differences in the percentage of each group having collateral reports of impairment on the IRS were not significant ($\chi^2 = 19.38$, $df = 12$, p = NS). The collaterals were typically parents (ADHD = 67%, Clinical = 44%, and Community = 53%). The remaining collaterals were spouses/partners, friends, or siblings or the participants. Examination of the patterns of relationships of these other people to the participants across the groups revealed no significant differences.

For the entire sample of participants in this study, the agreement between self and others was reasonable or satisfactory ($r = .68$, $p < .001$, $N = 184$). When we examined agreement on specific domains, we found the following correlations: home life (.55), work (.48), social interactions (.38), community activities (.28), education (.68), marriage/dating (.62), money management (.60), driving (.47), leisure activities (.38) (note that this domain has no equivalent on the BFIS), and daily responsibilities (.55). On the one hand, these correlations would be expected to be lower than those for the BFIS because the item response scaling was truncated to just a 0–3 rating instead of the 0–9 scaling on the BFIS. On the other hand, the oversampling of clinic-referred patients in the UMASS Study (two of the three patient groups were clinical populations) would be expected to create a far wider range of ratings of impairment and an overemphasis on more severe ratings than in a general population sample, and this would be expected to inflate the correlations so obtained.

In a separate study, known as the Milwaukee Study, large samples of hyperactive children ($n = 158$) and control children ($n = 81$) were followed to adulthood (mean age 27 years) (Barkley et al., 2008). At that follow-up, the IRS was administered. Ratings were also obtained from others who knew these children well, primarily parents again. The degree of agreement in the Total Impairment Score for the IRS was .43, which was considerably lower than that obtained in the UMASS Study. This can probably be attributed to the younger age of the Milwaukee sample, relative to the older adults used in the UMASS Study. Research on ADHD suggests that young adults' ratings of their symptoms show greater disparities or lower agreement with the ratings of others who know them well (Barkley et al., in press). This implies a growing degree of agreement between adults with ADHD and others as the adults reach at least 30 years of age. In both the UMASS and Milwaukee Studies, comparisons of the group means for the self-reported impairment ratings to those for the reports of others show relatively similar levels of agreement, as can be seen in Figures 5.1 and 5.2. In the Milwaukee Study, others reported on average a greater degree of impairment in these young adults than did the young adults themselves; in the UMASS Study, adults reported the same impairment as, or slightly more impairment than, others who knew them well did.

In the UMASS Study, the average disparities or differences between the mean ratings provided by the adults and the mean ratings provided by others were relatively modest (ADHD = 1.05, Clinical = 2.50, and Community = –0.04), which might indicate close agreement. Indeed, the groups did not differ from each other in

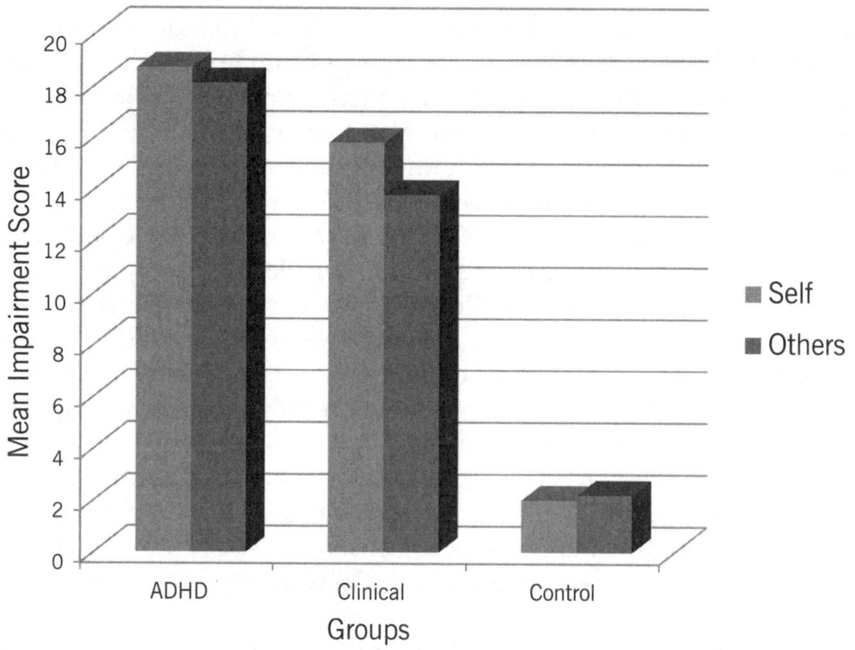

FIGURE 5.1. Comparison of self-ratings and other-ratings of impairment in 10 major life activities for adults with ADHD, a Clinical control group of adults, and adults in a Community control group from the UMASS Study. Data from Barkley et al. (2008).

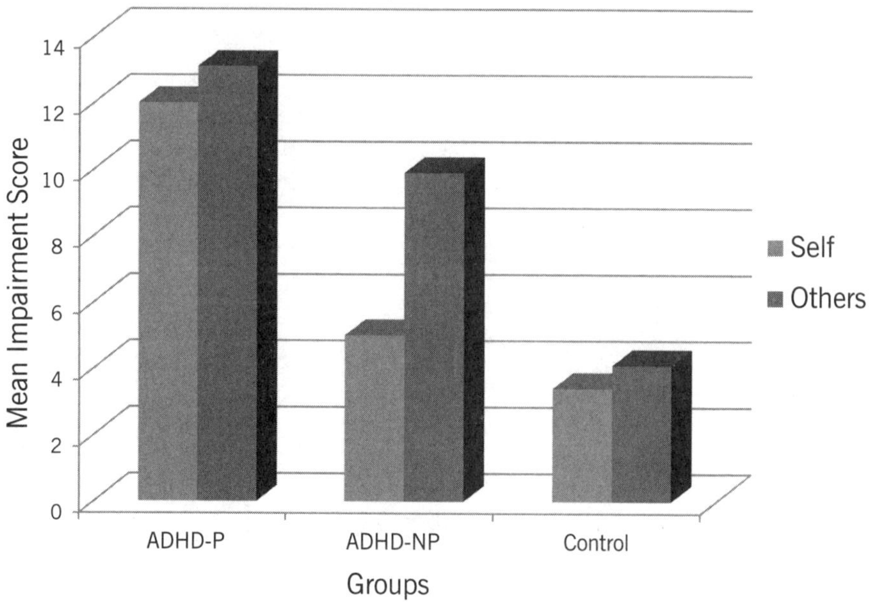

FIGURE 5.2. Comparison of self-ratings and other-ratings of impairment in 10 major life activities for hyperactive children whose ADHD had persisted to age 27 (ADHD-P), those whose ADHD had not persisted (ADHD-NP), and a control group followed concurrently to adulthood from the Milwaukee Study of hyperactive children as adults. Data from Barkley et al. (2008).

this respect (see Barkley et al., 2008). But the standard deviations for these groups were sizeable (ADHD = 7.82, Clinical = 7.08, and Community = 5.61), indicating a considerable range of disparities between these sources in their ratings of the participants' degree of impairment. Note also that disparities were far larger in both Clinical groups than in the Community group; this obviously has to do with the greater degree of impairment likely to exist in such Clinical groups, and hence the greater opportunity for disagreement and for more extensive disagreement or disparity. We (Barkley et al., in press) found that the degree of disparity was not so much related to intelligence or education as to the degree of ADHD, anxiety, and (to a lesser extent) depression. Hence, in cases where disparities in impairment ratings between patients and others who know them well are sizeable (greater than 1.5 *SD*s above the mean), clinicians should explore the possible existence of these disorders as explanations for such disparities.

In fact, self–other disparities above the 1.5-*SD* threshold should be a reason to explore all possible bases for such large disparities. This does not mean that one source (other-ratings) should always be construed as the gold standard against which to judge the truthfulness or accuracy of self-ratings. But an interview with either or both parties should be conducted to determine why such large disparities have been found. Of course, another possibility to pursue is that a participant may be malingering so as to gain some immediate benefit from a diagnosis of a psychiatric disorder, such as accommodations in a college setting (Booksh, Pella, Singh, & Gouvier, 2010; Harrison, Edwards, & Parker, 2007) or on professional examinations; an insurance settlement; or more lenient criminal sentencing in a court (Murphy & Gordon, 2006).

CHAPTER 6

Validity

The term "validity" is usually taken to mean the accuracy, correctness, or truth value of an assertion or conclusion (Bryant, 2000), as typically measured against the empirical evidence in support of or refuting the assertion and against the logical basis for that assertion or conclusion. It is therefore the degree to which some truth claim conforms to the evidence of reality. In scale development, the term means the extent to which the measure does what it claims to do. Here it refers specifically to the degree to which the BFIS evaluates psychosocial impairment. Some initial work has been done on validating the BFIS; some was also done with its prototype, the IRS (see Chapter 2). Both sets of research are discussed here.

Construct Validity

Face Validity

Establishing construct validity begins with a clear and explicit definition of the construct that a measure is intended to assess (Bryant, 2000; Cook & Campbell, 1979). Without such a definition, it is not possible to evaluate a rating scale to determine whether its items are correctly sampling from and hence evaluating the conceptual domain of this construct. The construct measured by the BFIS is "psychosocial impairment." Impairment has been defined in Chapter 1 of this manual as the extent of difficulty an individual experiences in functioning effectively in a major domain of human life activity. It is considered a dimensional construct, in that humans are believed to vary in their degree of functional ineffectiveness in performing major life activities. The functional major life domains assessed by the BFIS include self-care routines, childrearing, education, work, and 11 others (see Chapter 3 and the Appendix). This form of construct validity is usually considered face validity: To what degree do the items on the scale appear to sample the construct (its semantic content or meaning) they are intended to assess? The BFIS must be viewed as having high face validity because (1) the instructions direct respondents to evaluate their performance (or the index persons' performance, in the Other-Report versions) in 15 major domains of psychosocial functioning; and (2) the respondents are directed to rate their (or the index persons') degree of difficulty functioning effectively in those domains, or the degree to which they experience impairment. The definition of the construct and the major life domains it refers to are explicit in the content of the scale.

Multitrait, Multimethod Evidence

Once a construct has been appropriately specified, a second approach to evaluating its construct validity is to compare ratings on the scale to ratings on another measure of that same construct. Presumably, if both scales are evaluating the same construct, then the two measures should be more highly correlated with each other than either is with measures of different constructs. Such an analysis may include a multitrait, multimethod matrix of measures evaluating similar and dissimilar constructs. Table 6.1 provides an example of such a matrix. It shows the correlations among two measures each for four distinct constructs: impairment, verbal working memory, inattention, and occupational status. The data are taken from the large UMASS Study of adults with ADHD, adults in a Clinical control group, and those in a Community control group as discussed in Chapter 5 (see Barkley et al., 2008). This correlation matrix obviously illustrates the construct validity of the IRS, which was the precursor to the current BFIS. The self-ratings of impairment on the IRS

TABLE 6.1. Multitrait, Multimethod Matrix for Measures of Impairment, Working Memory, and Inattention from the UMASS Study of Adult ADHD

Construct/measure	1	2	3	4	5	6	7	8
Impairment								
1. IRS (self-rating)	—							
2. SOFAS (clinician rating)	**–.74**	—						
Verbal working memory								
3. Digit Span Forward (LAMB)	–.16	.14	—					
4. Digit Span Backward (LAMB)	–.13	.15	**.56**	—				
Inattention								
5. CPT Omissions	.12	–.16	–.03	–.08	—			
6. CPT Reaction Time Variability	.22	–.22	–.05	–.13	**.51**	—		
Occupational status								
7. Hollingshead job index	–.02	.19	.08	.03	–.15	–.16	—	
8. Current salary	.11	.05	.06	.07	–.10	–.10	**.50**	—

Note. SOFAS, Social and Occupational Functioning Assessment Scale; LAMB, Learning and Memory Battery; CPT, Conners' Continuous Performance Test. See Barkley et al. (2008) for descriptions of these measures.

and the clinician SOFAS rating (see Chapter 1) were far more highly correlated with each other (shown in bold type) than they were with the other measures of the other constructs. The same was true for each pair of measures of the other constructs: In each pair, one measure was more highly correlated with the other measure of that construct than either scale happened to be with the measures of the other constructs. The results show that impairment measures are distinct from those of verbal working memory, inattention, and occupational status.

As Table 6.1 also illustrates, the self-ratings of impairment in the 10 different domains of major life activities measured on the IRS shared nearly 55% of the variance with the clinician rating of impairment in social and occupational functioning on the SOFAS. The BFIS contains 9 of the 10 domains assessed in the IRS, as well as 5 domains not evaluated in the IRS. And the BFIS also provides a broader range of ratings for each domain (0–9) than the range in the IRS (0–4). Both of these characteristics would have produced a more limited range of scores for the IRS than for its descendant scale, the BFIS. As such, not only does the evidence of validity for the IRS have a direct bearing on the validity of the BFIS, but such evidence is likely to be of less magnitude than would have been obtained if the BFIS had been used in its place in such analyses.

Interobserver Agreement

Evidence for the construct validity of the BFIS can also be found in the results for interobserver agreement reported in Chapter 5. Do the evaluations provided by two people on the same instrument evaluating the same person yield an acceptable degree of agreement on the construct(s) being rated? As reported in that chapter, the correlation was a respectable .68 for the IRS in the UMASS Study.

Factor Analysis

Some additional evidence for the construct validity of the BFIS comes from the results of the factor analysis described in Chapter 3. As described there, it was found that the 15 domains on the BFIS constitute a single factor that accounts for more than 50% of the variance in the impairment ratings across these domains. This also makes it evident that individuals having difficulties with functioning effectively in any particular domain are highly likely to be having such difficulties functioning in the other domains assessed on the BFIS. Degree of functional ineffectiveness is obviously somewhat domain-specific, given the other setting-specific variables that are likely to affect a particular domain of major life activity. Yet it is clear from these results that a general factor of impairment or functional ineffectiveness also underlies all of these domains of major human life activities—much as the general intelligence factor, *g*, has been found to exist across all specific intelligence scale subtests.

Another way to demonstrate that the psychological dimension being assessed by the BFIS is distinct from other constructs is to conduct a factor analysis entering the scores from the BFIS along with scores from other measures believed to measure other constructs. This is similar to the multitrait, multimethod matrix shown in Table 6.1, in that the aim is to demonstrate the relative independence of measures of one construct from measures of another. The Barkley Deficits in Executive Functioning Scale (BDEFS; Barkley, 2011b) and the Barkley Adult ADHD Rating Scale–IV (BAARS-IV; Barkley, 2011a) were both administered to the normative sample. The five scores from the BDEFS and two scores from the BAARS-IV (Inattentive, Hyperactive–Impulsive) were entered along with the 15 BFIS domain ratings into a principal component factor analysis with varimax rotation. Results indicated two distinct factors. The first, accounting for 48.8% of the variance prior to rotation (33.9% after rotation), was the BFIS Adaptive–Social Impairment factor (eigenvalue = 10.73) consisting of all 15 domain ratings (all loadings ranged from .540 to .747 on this factor and from .215 to .360 on the second factor). The second factor (eigenvalue = 2.05) accounted for an additional 8.3% of variance (24.2% after rotation) and consisted of the BDEFS and BAARS-IV scores (factor loadings ranged from .700 to .842 on this factor and from .112 to .397 on the first factor). It is not surprising that these scores formed a single factor, as ADHD is known to involve substantial deficits in executive functioning (EF) and may well be a disorder of EF (Barkley, 1997; Barkley & Murphy, in press). This evidence is consistent with the notion that impairment constitutes a separate construct from disorders—in this case, ADHD and EF deficits.

A similar analysis was conducted for the present manual, using the data from the UMASS Study of adults with ADHD and two control groups (Barkley et al., 2008). This time, the 10 domain ratings from the IRS were submitted to a factor analysis, along with the 10 subscales of various dimensions of psychopathology assessed by the Symptom Checklist 90—Revised (SCL-90-R; Derogatis, 1986): Depression, Anxiety, Somatization, Complaints, Obsessive–Compulsive, Interpersonal Sensitivity, Hostility, Phobic Anxiety, Paranoid Ideation, and Psychoticism. A PCFA was conducted on these scores, using the entire sample of participants and a varimax rotation. Results revealed two distinct factors. The first factor (eigenvalue = 11.10) constituted a Psychopathology factor that captured 58.4% of the variance before rotation (35.4% afterward) and contained all nine of the SCL-90-R scores, with factor loadings ranging from .731 (Somatization) to .863 (Interpersonal Sensitivity). The second factor contained the 10 ratings from the IRS, which constituted an Impairment factor (eigenvalue = 2.03) accounting for 10.7% of the variance before rotation (33.7% afterward), with factor loadings ranging from .573 (driving) to .810 (daily responsibilities).

An identical analysis was conducted for the present manual, using the large dataset from the Milwaukee Study of hyperactive and control children followed into adulthood (see Barkley et al., 2008). A PCFA was conducted on the adult follow-up data, using the same 10 domain ratings from the IRS and the 10 SCL-90-R psychopathology scales. The results were virtually the same as those from the UMASS Study. A two-factor solution emerged, with the first factor representing the SCL-90-R scales (eigenvalue = 9.61) and explaining 50.6% of the variance before rotation, with factor loadings ranging from .689 (Phobic Anxiety) to .844 (Paranoid Ideation). The second factor was an Impairment factor containing all 10 domain ratings from the IRS (eigenvalue = 2.00), explaining another 10.5% of variance, and having loadings ranging from .602 (driving) to .774 (daily responsibilities). Thus the construct of impairment is not only distinct from those of EF and ADHD, as shown above; it is also distinct from one comprising general psychopathology.

Disability Status

Still further evidence for construct validity can be found in comparisons among individuals with regard to their work disability status. Information was collected on the employment status of the normative sample reported in this manual. These categories of employment were compared to each other, using one-way analysis of variance on the Mean Impairment Score of the BFIS. The results were significant for the BFIS-LF ($F = 18.13$, $p < .001$) as well as for the BFIS Quick Screen ($F = 19.00$, $p < .001$). Findings for both measures appear in Figure 6.1. Pairwise comparisons indicated that those individuals classified as not working due to disability had significantly higher impairment ratings than those in all other work categories had. Individuals currently on temporary layoff or looking for work had the next highest mean ratings, which, though placing below the level for disabled workers, were higher than those for individuals who were currently employed, retired, or not working for other reasons (usually stay-at-home parents). Interestingly, retirees reported the lowest levels of impairment—most likely because they no longer had to function in several important domains, such as work, education, and childrearing.

Corresponding results for the Percent Domains Impaired scores for both versions of the BFIS are shown in Figure 6.2. The one-way analysis of variance on the Percent Domains Impaired score for these work categories was significant for the BFIS-LF ($F = 18.78$, $p < .001$) as well as for the BFIS Quick Screen ($F = 20.71$, $p <$ 001). Those participants classified as disabled reported being impaired in more

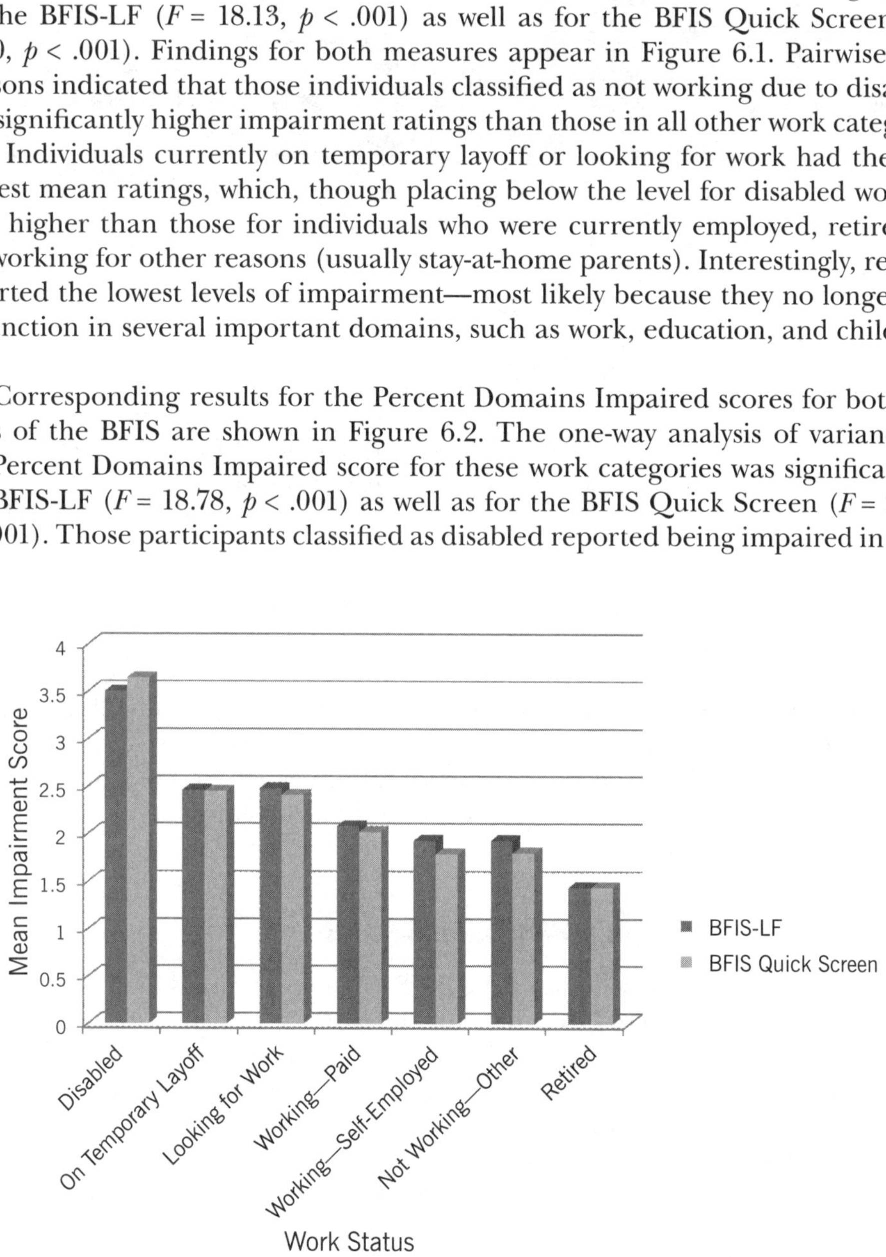

FIGURE 6.1. Mean Impairment Scores from the BFIS-LF and BFIS Quick Screen versions for seven different work status categories in the normative sample.

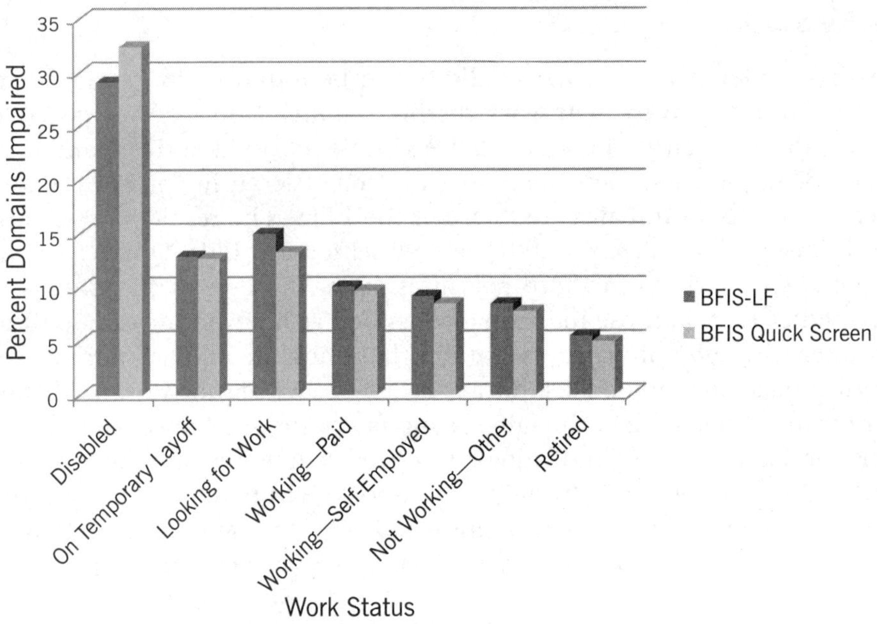

FIGURE 6.2. Percent Domains Impaired scores from the BFIS-LF and BFIS Quick Screen for seven different work status categories in the normative sample.

domains than participants in any other work status categories reported. The disabled individuals reported being impaired in more than twice as many domains as individuals currently employed, and nearly five times as many as retirees. Those looking for work reported impairment in a higher percentage of domains than did those currently employed, those not working for other reasons (e.g., homemakers), and retirees. This was also the case for this same score from the BFIS Quick Screen. The BFIS therefore has satisfactory validity when judged against an individual's current work disability status.

Ratings of Impairment in Individual Domains

Evidence for the construct validity of the BFIS can also be found in examination of its individual domain ratings and their relationship to other measures that would indicate impairment in that domain. Not all BFIS domains had evidence available that could speak to their validity, but evidence was available from the normative sample and from earlier studies using the prototype IRS for the domains of work, education, marriage/cohabiting/dating, driving, money management, daily responsibilities, and health maintenance. That evidence is examined below. No evidence was available concerning the validity of the impairment ratings for the remaining domains on the BFIS, such as childrearing, sexual relations, community activities, social–friends, or social–strangers. Future research will need to examine those domains for the validity of their impairment ratings. Yet where evidence is available, it indicates that specific domain ratings have construct validity.

Work Impairment

For instance, a comparison can be made among the work status groups in the normative sample (see above) on their ratings for the specific domain of work on the BFIS. Again, recall that this domain is rated for degree of impairment on a 0–9 Likert scale. The same results were obtained as described above for the more general Mean Impairment Scores ($F = 4.47$, $p < .001$). Individuals who were classified as disabled from work reported nearly twice as much impairment ($M = 3.9$, $SD = 3.2$) in the work domain as those currently working ($M = 1.95$, $SD = 2.1$), those in retirement ($M = 1.7$, $SD = 1.9$), those on layoff ($M = 2.1$, $SD = 2.2$), or those not working for other reasons such as homemaking ($M = 1.8$, $SD = 2.3$). They also reported themselves as more impaired than those not working but seeking employment ($M = 2.4$, $SD = 2.4$). The degree of rated impairment in the work domain is obviously related to disability status.

The validity for a specific single rating of work impairment can also be examined by using the IRS data collected in the UMASS Study of adult ADHD. In that study, various other measures of work history and functioning were collected from an interview with the participant; from the clinician rating on the SOFAS; and, in a subset of patients, from a rating scale completed by their workplace supervisors. The measure from the supervisors was especially important in providing yet another source besides the participants for data on their workplace functioning. In Table 6.2 are the Pearson correlations between the specific IRS work domain rating (as well as the IRS Total Impairment Score) and the various occupational functioning measures.

On the one hand, these correlations could be expected to be low because the IRS used just a 0–3 rating of impairment for each domain, whereas the BFIS uses a 0–9 rating; the former would be expected to limit the range of a potential correlation, compared to the latter. On the other hand, the UMASS Study over-recruited clinical patients, who would be expected to have more impairment, and so this might inflate the size of correlations relative to those that might be obtained in a general population sample. These factors were true for all of the remaining evidence derived from the IRS ratings in the UMASS Study, and so they are not repeated within the discussions below of the other specific domains of impairment. Table 6.2 clearly demonstrates that both the single rating of impairment in the specific domain of work and the Total Impairment Score across all 10 domains on the IRS were significantly related to most of the specific measures of occupational functioning across three different sources of information (self, clinician, employer). All these data suggest that a single rating of degree of impairment in the specific work domain, as provided on the BFIS (or the earlier IRS), has some validity when judged against other measures of occupational functioning.

Education Impairment

Evidence for the validity of the rating on the specific domain of education in the BFIS was obtained from the findings on the normative sample's educational status ($F = 12.77$, $p < .001$). Specifically, those with less than a high school education rated their impairment in this domain more than twice as high ($M = 3.6$, $SD = 3.0$) as did

TABLE 6.2. Correlations of Occupational Functioning Measures with the Specific Work Impairment Self-Rating and Total Impairment Score from the UMASS Study of Adults with ADHD

Occupational functioning measures (*n*'s)	Work impairment rating	Total Impairment Score
Employer measures		
Employer-rated work quality (97, 89)	.34*	.33*
Employer-rated workplace impairment (83, 75)	.30*	.20
Clinician rating		
Clinician SOFAS rating (301, 277)	–.63**	–.74**
Self-reported work history		
Number of jobs held since high school (292, 266)	.20**	.20**
Self-rated quality of work (228, 206)	.35**	.29**
Percent of jobs where person had trouble getting along with others (299, 272)	.28**	.30**
Percent of jobs where person had trouble with own behavior or work performance (289, 263)	.42**	.48**
Percent of jobs from which person was fired(290, 264)	.22**	.26**
Percent of jobs where person quit due to hostility with employer (291, 265)	.19**	.24**
Percent of jobs where person quit due to boredom (290, 264)	.13	.17*
Percent of jobs in which was disciplined for substandard work (291, 265)	.19**	.25**

Note. n = sample sizes for each correlation in that row, respectively; SOFAS, Social and Occupational Functioning Assessment Scale.
*$p < .01$; **$p < .001$.

those who had at least a bachelor's degree ($M = 1.5$, $SD = 2.0$), and also rated themselves as significantly more impaired than those with a high school education ($M = 2.6$, $SD = 2.7$) or those with some college ($M = 2.6$, $SD = 2.7$). Those having just a high school education also reported higher impairment in this domain than those having at least a bachelor's degree, and those with some college also reported higher impairment than those with a bachelor's degree or higher. Degree of rated impairment in the education domain on the BFIS is thus clearly related to the degree of education obtained in the normative sample.

A similar pattern emerged in comparisons of the Mean Impairment Scores for these educational groups on both the BFIS-LF ($F = 9.96$, $p < .001$) and the BFIS Quick Screen ($F = 10.29$, $p < .001$), as shown in Figure 6.3; it also emerged on the Percent Domains Impaired scores for these groups, as displayed in Figure 6.4 (BFIS-LF: $F = 11.57$, $p < .001$; BFIS Quick Screen: $F = 10.27$, $p < .001$). For the Mean Impairment Score on the BFIS-LF, for instance, pairwise comparisons showed the following results: less than high school > high school, some college, and bachelor's degree or higher; high school > bachelor's degree or higher; and some college > bachelor's degree or higher. This pattern of contrasts was found for the other scores as well.

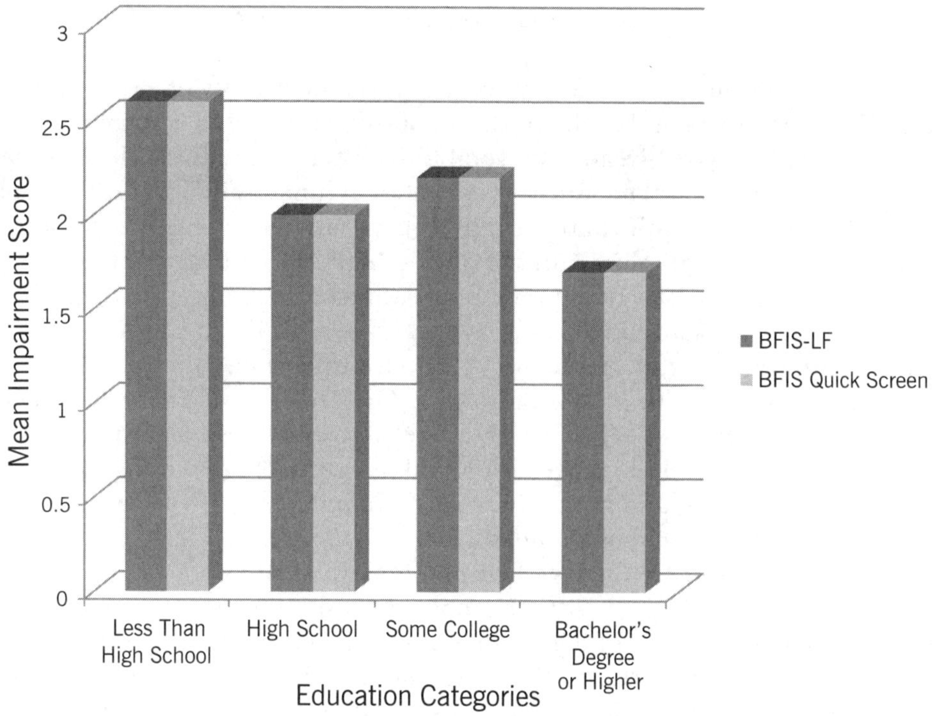

FIGURE 6.3. Mean Impairment Scores from the BFIS-LF and BFIS Quick Screen for four different education categories in the normative sample.

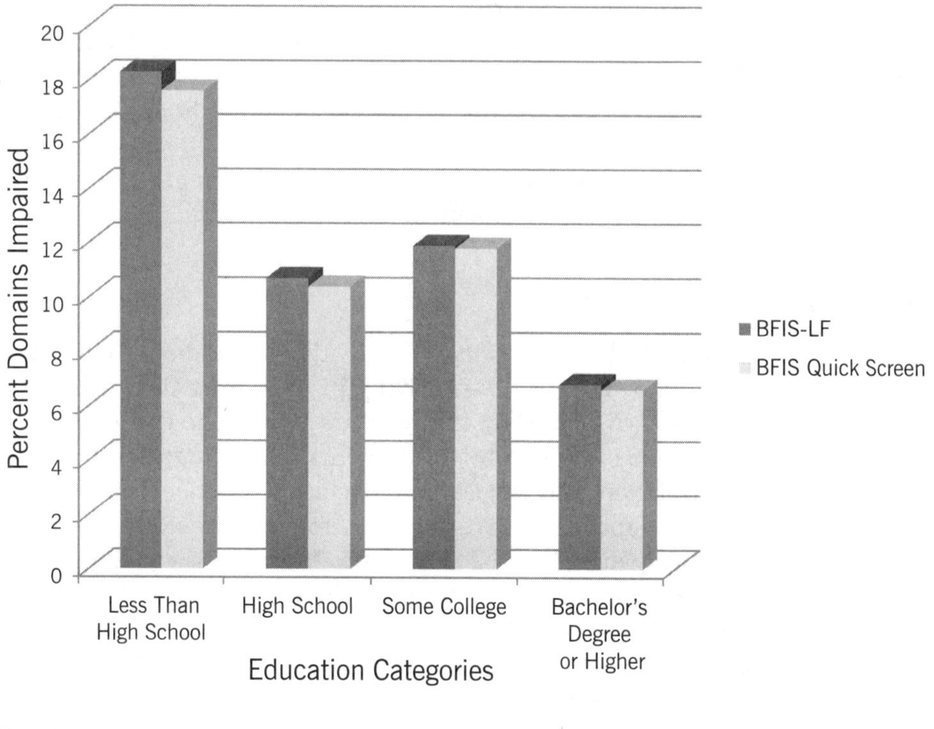

FIGURE 6.4. Percent Domains Impaired scores from the BFIS-LF and BFIS Quick Screen for four different education categories in the normative sample.

Evidence from the UMASS Study also supports the validity of a specific rating of educational impairment. For the purposes of this manual, the education domain score from the prototype IRS and the Total Impairment Score from all 10 domains were correlated with several measures of educational functioning. Self-rated impairment in education was significantly negatively correlated with years of education ($r = -.25$, $p < .001$, $n = 306$); class ranking on the high school transcript ($r = -.28$, $p = .002$, $n = 122$); and high school grade point average from that transcript for the last year of high school attended ($r = -.30$, $p < .001$, $n = 245$). It was also positively correlated with self-reported frequency of school suspensions ($r = .13$, $p = .028$, $n = 306$) and truancies ($r = .19$, $p = .001$, $n = 305$). The Total Impairment Score across all 10 domains was likewise significantly correlated with these measures: years of education ($r = -.15$, $p = .014$, $n = 281$); class ranking on the high school transcript ($r = -.35$, $p < .001$, $n = 113$); and high school grade point average from that transcript for the last year of high school attended ($r = -.34$, $p < .001$, $n = 224$). It was significantly related as well to frequency of suspensions ($r = .20$, $p = .001$, $n = 281$) and truancies ($r = .19$, $p = .001$, $n = 281$). Here we see a significant set of relationships between a simple 0–3 rating of educational impairment and three relatively objective measures—ones based not on the same source (self-report) as the impairment rating, but on official archival records (transcripts).

In this same study, participants were asked about problems in their educational history. These were dichotomous (yes–no) questions. For this manual, the IRS education domain ratings of those who had experienced these adverse events and those who had not were compared. For instance, individuals who reported having been retained in a grade at least once reported significantly higher impairment in the education domain of the IRS ($M = 2.3$, $SD = 1.0$) than did those who were not retained ($M = 1.6$, $SD = 1.2$) ($F = 12.52$, $p < .001$). This was also the case for those who reported having received special educational services in school ($M = 2.2$, $SD = 0.9$) versus those who did not ($M = 1.6$, $SD = 1.2$) ($F = 13.35$, $p < .001$). These findings provide additional evidence for the validity of the specific domain rating of education impairment (as well as for the impairment summary score).

Impairment in Money Management

Another specific domain of the BFIS calls for individuals to report the degree of functional difficulty (impairment) they are having in managing their money (and general finances, such as paying bills, handling credit, etc.). The construct validity of this specific rating can be evaluated by using the income categories that existed in the normative sample. There was a clear linear relationship between the degree of current annual income and the degree of functional difficulty people in the sample reported in this domain ($F = 7.52$, $p < .001$). Individuals earning less than $20,000 per year reported more impairment in this domain ($M = 2.8$, $SD = 2.7$) than did those who earned $20,000–39,999 ($M = 2.2$, $SD = 2.5$), those earning $40,000–74,999 ($M = 2.1$, $SD = 2.3$), those earning $75,000–99,999 ($M = 1.8$, $SD = 2.2$), or those earning $100,000 or more ($M = 1.5$, $SD = 2.0$). The pairwise contrasts showed the following significant differences in impairment ratings among these categories: less than $20,000 > all other income categories; $20,000–$39,999 > $75,000–99,999, $100,000; and $40,000–$74,999 > $100,000. Degree of functional impairment in the money management domain of the BFIS is thus obviously related to degree of annual income in the normative sample, giving clear evidence for the construct validity of this domain rating.

This relationship was also evident in the Mean Impairment Scores (see Figure 6.5) and Percent Domains Impaired scores (Figure 6.6) from both versions of the BFIS. That is, a lower degree of annual income was associated with greater mean impairment ratings across all domains, as well as with a greater percentage of domains rated in the impaired range. The greatest impairment and the greatest pervasiveness of impairment across domains were most evident in the group making less than $20,000 per year.

As with the domains described above, some evidence for the validity of the specific rating of impairment in the money management domain can be gleaned from the UMASS Study, which used the IRS and also collected information about a history of financial management problems from its participants (Barkley et al., 2008). For this manual, the 0–3 IRS rating of money management problems was correlated with various problems in managing money reported during a clinical interview. The following results were obtained for reports of the frequency with which these events had occurred: missed rent payments ($r = .20$, $p = .001$, $n = 270$); missed utility payments and had services discontinued as a result ($r = .13$, $p = .028$, $n = 274$); missed loan payments ($r = .18$, $p = .002$, $n = 270$); exceeded credit card limit ($r = .19$, $p = .001$, $n = 265$); wrote checks for insufficient funds ($r = .18$, $p = .002$, $n = 289$); and had a low self-reported credit rating ($r = .42$, $p < .001$, $n = 288$). These correla-

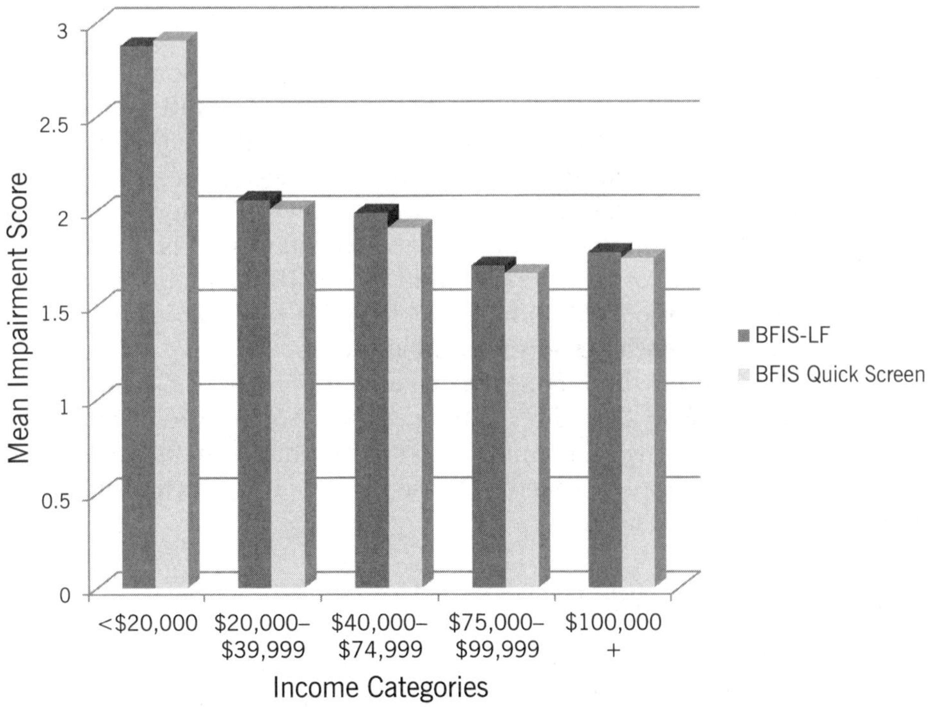

FIGURE 6.5. Mean Impairment Scores from the BFIS-LF and BFIS Quick Screen for five different income categories in the normative sample.

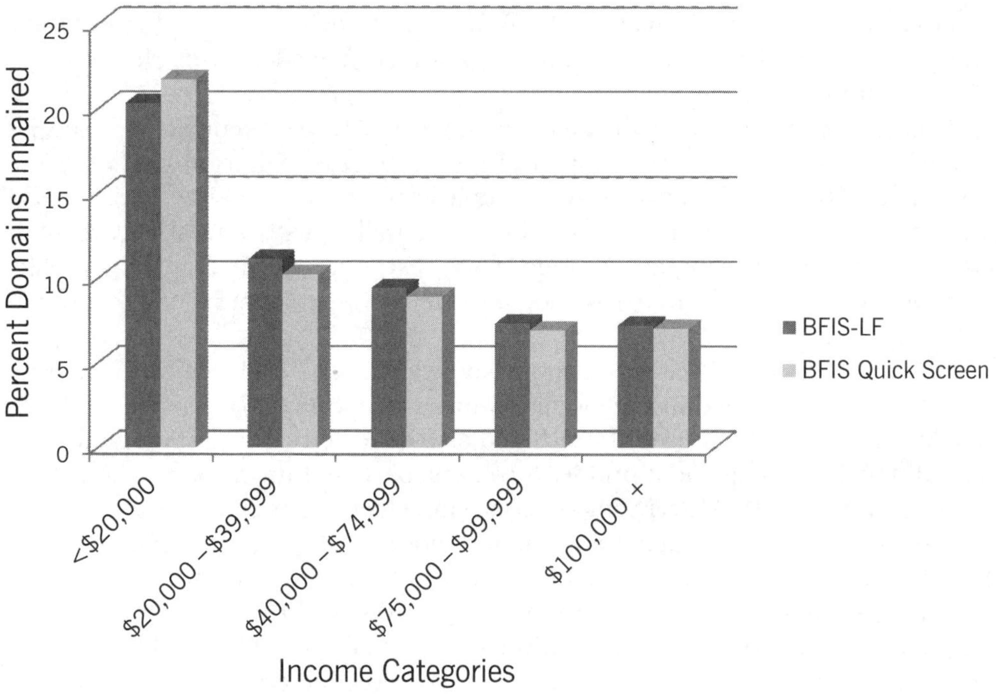

FIGURE 6.6. Percent Domains Impaired scores from the BFIS-LF and BFIS Quick Screen for five different income categories in the normative sample.

tions are certainly of a low, though significant, magnitude in most cases. Yet they do provide some evidence for the credibility of the impairment rating in the money management domain, especially in the relationship with the self-reported credit rating; these two measures shared over 16% of their variance. Categorical measures of money problems were also available from this interview. Those results indicated that individuals who stated in the interview that they had problems managing their money also rated themselves as more impaired in this IRS domain (M = 2.3, SD = 0.9) than did those who reported no such problems (M = 0.7, SD = 0.9) (F = 212.57, p < .002). Likewise, those who reported trouble saving money (M = 2.2, SD = 1.0) gave a higher rating of impaired money management than did those not reporting such trouble (M = 0.8, SD = 0.9) (F = 159.05, p < .001). Finally, those who reported having problems with buying on impulse also reported higher money management impairment (M = 2.2, SD = 1.0) than did those not reporting such problems (M = 0.8, SD = 1.0) (F = 140.87, p < .001).

Marriage/Cohabiting/Dating Impairment

Another specific BFIS domain pertains to the degree of difficulty individuals may be experiencing in their marriage, cohabiting, or dating relationships—in other words, their intimate living relationships. If this rating has some construct validity, then differences in rated impairment should be evident across the marital status groupings in the normative sample. Indeed, such significant differences were found even after age was controlled for ($F = 10.60$, $p < .001$). Those who were currently separated ($M = 3.2$, $SD = 2.5$), divorced ($M = 3.1$, $SD = 2.8$), never married ($M = 3.2$, $SD = 3.0$), or living with a partner ($M = 2.7$, $SD = 2.4$) reported significantly higher levels of impairment in this domain than did individuals who were currently married ($M = 1.9$, $SD = 2.1$) or were widowed ($M = 2.0$, $SD = 2.6$). The former groupings did not differ from each other, nor did those in the latter two groupings. Again, such findings provide evidence for the validity of the rating in this domain. And, just as with the other specific domains above, evidence was also obtained for a more generalized form of impairment, in that individuals in the first set of living arrangements reported overall higher Mean Impairment Scores on both the BFIS-LF and BFIS Quick Screen than did those who were married or widowed. This was also true for the Percent Domains Impaired scores on both versions of the BFIS. The results for both sets of scores appear in Figures 6.7 and 6.8, respectively.

Additional evidence for the validity of the impairment rating in this domain of major life activity comes from the UMASS Study, in which individuals were asked to rate the degree of their marital satisfaction on the Locke–Wallace Marital Adjustment Test (Locke & Wallace, 1959). Similar ratings were also obtained from their cohabiting partners, whether they were formally married or not. The correlations between the impairment rating for the domain of marriage and dating (as it was called in the IRS) and the Locke–Wallace scale were as follows: self-rated marital satisfaction ($r = -.38$, $p < .001$, $n = 127$) and spouse/partner-rated marital satisfaction ($r = -.45$, $p < .001$, $n = 119$). Thus, in general, the specific BFIS domain of marriage/cohabiting/dating has evidence for its construct validity.

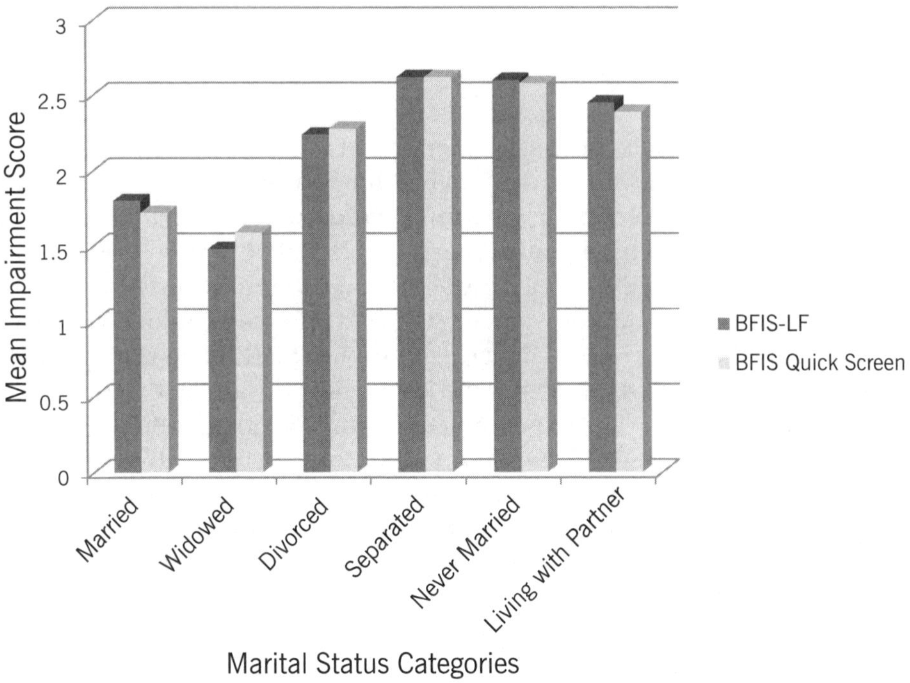

FIGURE 6.7. Mean Impairment Scores from the BFIS-LF and BFIS Quick Screen for six different marital status categories in the normative sample.

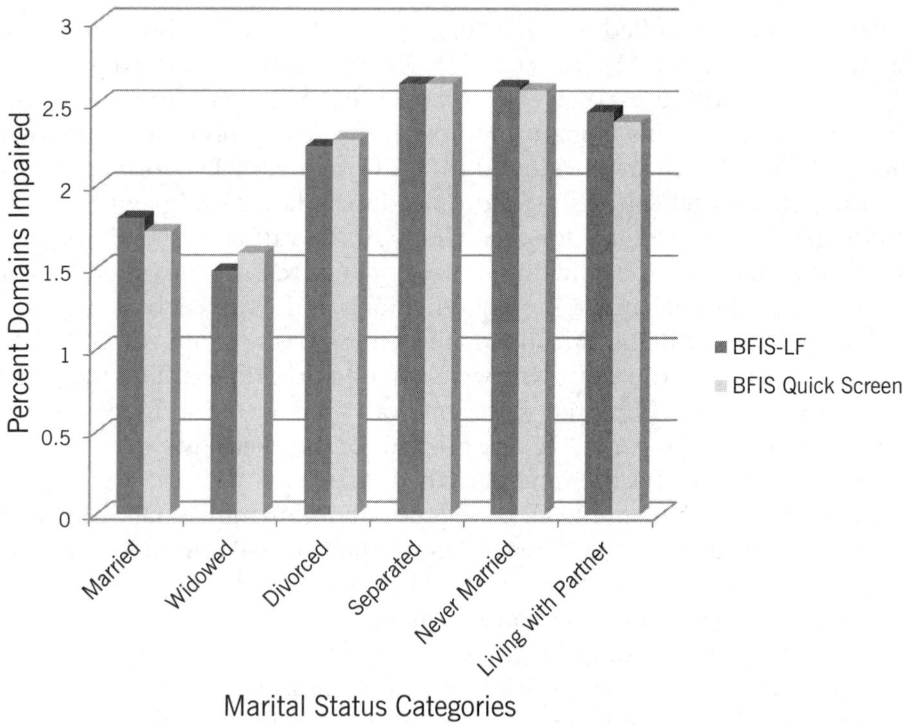

FIGURE 6.8. Percent Domains Impaired scores from the BFIS-LF and BFIS Quick Screen for six different marital status categories in the normative sample.

Driving Impairment

No information is available about the extent to which participants in the normative sample had problems with driving that could be used to validate their rating of impairment in this BFIS domain. But information was collected in the UMASS Study concerning adverse driving outcomes, as reflected both in self-reported driving history during an interview and on the official driving records from the Massachusetts Department of Motor Vehicles (DMV). The correlations between the self-rated degree of driving impairment on the prototype IRS and the self-reported frequency of adverse driving outcomes during a clinical interview were as follows: crashes ($r = .28$, $p < .001$, $n = 306$); speeding citations ($r = .30$, $p < .001$, $n = 306$); citations for reckless driving ($r = .17$, $p = .003$, $n = 306$); citations for driving under the influence of alcohol ($r = .21$, $p < .001$, $n = 306$); citations for being at fault in crashes ($r = .35$, $p < .001$, $n = 306$); and frequency of license suspensions/revocations ($r = .23$, $p < .001$, $n = 305$). The number of citations recorded on the official DMV record was also significantly correlated with the self-rating of driving impairment on the IRS ($r = .18$, $p = .003$, $n = 272$), as was the number of crashes recorded on that record ($r = .14$, $p = .022$, $n = 272$). DMV records have been found not to be as accurate as self-reported driving history measures in driving research (see Barkley et al., 2008), and so it is not surprising that the correlations are somewhat lower for the DMV information than for the self-reported driving history measures. Even so, this information indicates some degree of validity or credibility for the driving domain in the IRS and, by inference, in the BFIS.

In a separate study examining the effects of alcohol on the driving performance of adults with ADHD and control adults, participants completed the IRS at baseline, along with a rating scale of safe driving behavior (Barkley, Murphy, O'Connell, Anderson, & Connor, 2006). The Driving Behavior Scale has been used in a variety of studies and has been found to be among the best predictors of adverse driving outcomes as reflected in self-reported driving history and official driving records (see Barkley & Cox, 2007). For this manual, a correlation was computed between the Total Impairment Score from the IRS and the total score for this driving scale ($r = -.62$, $p < .001$, $n = 102$). Higher self-rated Total Impairment Scores were clearly related to lower scores on the Driving Behavior Scale. Here is additional evidence that self-ratings of impairment are related to other measures of impairment in specific domains—in this case, driving a motor vehicle.

Impairment in Daily Responsibilities

Specific measures against which to validate the BFIS domain of daily responsibilities are difficult to come by. But management of day-to-day responsibilities would seem to have a great deal to do with EF, or one's capacity for self-regulation and problem solving across time to achieve one's goals. As noted earlier, ratings of EF were collected on the normative sample with the BDEFS, which evaluates five dimensions of EF deficits. The correlations between the self-rated degree of impairment on the daily responsibilities domain of the BFIS and the BDEFS subscales for these five EF dimensions were as follows: Self-Organization/Problem Solving ($r = .53$, $p < .001$, $n = 1{,}197$); Self-Management to Time ($r = .62$, $p < .001$, $n = 1{,}197$); Self-Discipline ($r = .45$, $p < .001$, $n = 1{,}197$); Self-Motivation ($r = .52$, $p < .001$, $n = 1{,}197$); and Self-Regulation of Emotions ($r = .47$, $p < .001$, $n = 1{,}197$).

Very similar results were obtained in the earlier UMASS Study of adults with ADHD (and other control groups), where the P-BDEFS, an earlier version of the BDEFS, was used. The correlations between the rating of the specific domain of daily responsibilities in the IRS and the P-BDEFS subscales were all high and significant: Self-Organization/Problem Solving ($r = .65$, $p < .001$, $n = 299$); Self-Management to Time ($r = .84$, $p < .001$, $n = 296$); Self-Discipline ($r = .71$, $p < .001$, $n = 279$); Self-Motivation ($r = .70$, $p < .001$, $n = 297$); and Self-Activation/Concentration ($r = .73$, $p < .001$, $n = 307$). The results for both of these large studies clearly support the idea that deficits in EF are highly associated with difficulties in effectively managing daily responsibilities, with the two sharing up to 70% of their variance in clinical samples and more than 36% of their variance in a general population sample. Both studies therefore attest to the validity of the impairment rating for this specific BFIS domain.

Impairment in Health Maintenance

No information was collected on health status or health maintenance activities in the normative sample to use in evaluating the validity of their impairment rating in this domain, but such information was available from the UMASS and Milwaukee

Studies. In the Milwaukee Study, this information was collected via the Skinner Health and Lifestyle Interview (Skinner, 1994). This interview examined the participants' lifestyle across 16 domains of health and categorized each domain as being a risk, a concern, or of no concern. These domains were nutrition, eating, caffeine use, physical fitness, weight, sleep, social functioning, family functioning, tobacco use, alcohol use, drug use, medication use, vehicle use, sexual functioning, work, and emotional health. The risk scores were summed across all 16 domains to create an overall Health Index for further examination here. This Health Index was then correlated with self-ratings of global impairment on the IRS and was found to be of moderate magnitude ($r = -.45$, $p < .001$, $n = 193$). A similar correlation was obtained between the IRS global rating and a measure of the total number of health problems endorsed during a medical status interview ($r = .41$, $p < .001$, $n = 196$). Thus, although no information about the validity of the specific rating of impairment in the health maintenance domain is available, evidence does indicate that the rating of overall impairment (to which the health maintenance domain was clearly related in the BFIS information discussed earlier; see Chapter 3) is certainly associated with greater medical problems and poorer health status. A similar relationship was observed in the UMASS Study, where the Health Index from the Skinner interview was significantly associated with self-rated global impairment on the IRS ($r = -.35$, $p < .001$, $n = 162$).

Discriminant Validity

As noted above, evidence for the validity of a measure can come from studies of its capacity to distinguish between psychiatrically disordered and nondisordered groups. One would expect that various psychiatric disorders would interfere with functioning in the domains rated on the BFIS. One disorder known to produce difficulties in functioning across nearly all of the domains examined on the BFIS is adult ADHD (see Barkley et al., 2008). Clinic-referred adults with ADHD, as well as children with ADHD who were followed to adulthood, have been found to have not only higher self-ratings of impairment but also higher ratings provided by others on the IRS. This is evident in Figure 5.1 (for the UMASS Study) and Figure 5.2 (for the Milwaukee Study) in Chapter 5. The UMASS Study showed that adults with ADHD, as well as clinic-referred adults with other disorders, had higher self-rated and other-rated IRS Total Impairment Scores than the Community control group had. The adults with ADHD also had higher scores than the Clinical control group. Similarly, hyperactive children whose ADHD persisted to young adulthood were rated by themselves and others on the IRS as more impaired than were those whose ADHD did not persist or those in the Community control group. The differences are not just evident on such global ratings; they were found on the vast majority of ratings of each specific domain of impairment. And these adults with ADHD have also been shown to be more impaired on various interview, archival, and psychometric measures of specific features of impairment within various domains of adaptive functioning, such as education, occupational functioning, peer relationships, driving, money management, marital satisfaction, health, antisocial behavior, substance use and abuse, criminal or antisocial activities, parenting stress, EF, and other domains (Barkley et al., 2008).

Further evidence of discriminant validity is apparent in the ratings of ADHD that were collected in the normative sample with the BAARS-IV (Barkley, 2011a). On this scale, the 18 symptoms of ADHD from DSM-IV-TR (American Psychiatric Association, 2000) are rated on a 0–3 Likert scale (not at all or rarely, sometimes, often, very often) and summed to create a total ADHD symptom score. In the normative sample, this total symptom score was found to be significantly and substantially correlated with every domain rated on the BFIS, and particularly with the summary scores. For instance, severity of ADHD correlated .62 ($p < .001$, $n = 1{,}232$) with the Mean Impairment Score from the BFIS-LF and .60 with this score from the BFIS Quick Screen. This shows that 36% of the variance or more in generalized impairment was accounted for by the severity of ADHD experienced in the normative sample. The severity of ADHD also correlated significantly with the Percent Domains Impairment score on both the BFIS-LF (.55) and the BFIS Quick Screen (.51) (all p's < .001). This demonstrates that the severity of ADHD shares more than 25% of the variance with the pervasiveness of impairment as assessed by the BFIS.

Another way to demonstrate discriminant validity is to break the normative sample into those who scored at the 95th percentile or above on the adult ADHD symptom ratings, and thus were at high risk for the diagnosis of the disorder; those scoring in the borderline ADHD range (84th–94th percentiles); and those placing in the normal range (<84th percentile). The comparisons on the Mean Impairment Scores and the Percent Domains Impaired scores for both BFIS versions were significant (F's = 183.95–236.10, all p's < .001). The results appear in Figure 6.9 for the Mean Impairment Scores and in Figure 6.10 for the Percent Domains Impaired scores, respectively. In all comparisons, the group scoring high on ADHD symptoms was rated as more impaired and more pervasively impaired than both the group with borderline ADHD scores and the normal group; the borderline group was also rated as more impaired than the normal group. Thus the BFIS is clearly detecting the significant and widespread impairment known to be associated with adult ADHD: As the severity of ADHD symptoms increases, so do ratings of both the severity and pervasiveness of impairment.

Criterion Validity

A further means of evaluating a measure for its usefulness in assessing a construct is its criterion validity. This refers to the relationship between a measure of a construct and measures of other criteria (constructs) that are hypothesized to be associated with or affected by that construct. For instance, Table 6.1 has shown self-rated impairment on the IRS to be highly correlated with clinician-rated impairment on the SOFAS.

No information is currently available on the value of the BFIS in predicting *future* outcomes, such as occupational, educational, financial, social, health, or even criminal outcomes. This would need to be evaluated in a longitudinal study that followed participants for a period of time after they had completed the BFIS and in

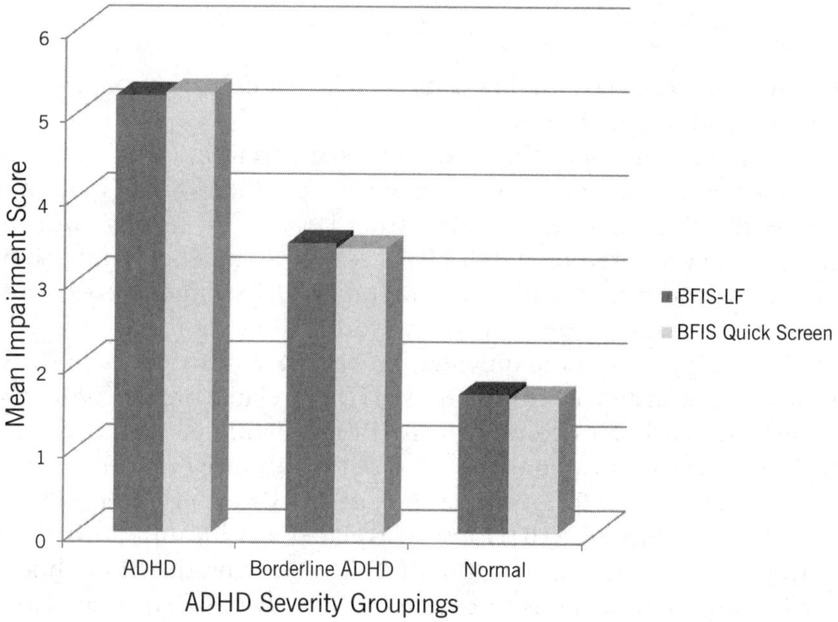

FIGURE 6.9. Mean Impairment Scores from the BFIS-LF and BFIS Quick Screen for three groups in the normative sample categorized by their scores on the BAARS-IV (Barkley, 2011a). ADHD, participants scoring at or above the 95th percentile; Borderline ADHD, participants scoring at the 84th–94th percentiles; Normal, participants scoring below the 84th percentile.

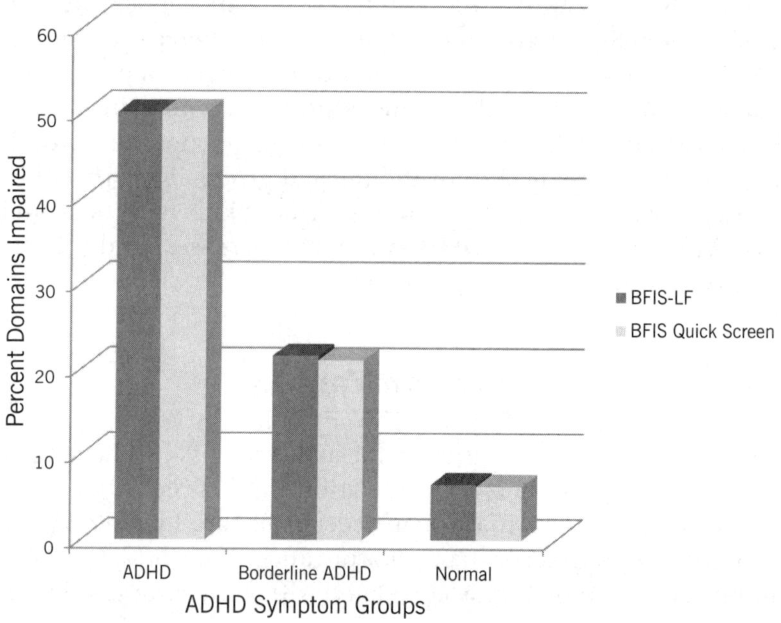

FIGURE 6.10. Percent Domains Impaired scores from the BFIS-LF and BFIS Quick Screen for three groups in the normative sample categorized by their scores on the BAARS-IV (Barkley, 2011a). ADHD, participants scoring at or above the 95th percentile; Borderline ADHD, participants scoring at the 84th–94th percentiles; Normal, participants scoring below the 84th percentile.

which various outcomes were measured. One could then examine how well baseline scores on the scale predicted these later outcomes. However, evidence is available on the concurrent validity of the scale—that is, how well it is associated with measures of outcomes collected at the same time that the BFIS (or its prototype, the IRS) was administered. Much of this evidence has been discussed above with regard to the specific relationship of BFIS ratings to education, work, income, disability status, and ADHD severity in the normative sample, as well as the evidence from the UMASS Study concerning the validity of the IRS ratings in the specific domains of work, marriage/dating, money management, driving, education, and daily responsibilities. The totality of evidence supports the validity of self-rated impairment as judged against other measures of impairment in those domains being rated.

Executive Functioning

EF is a metaconstruct or umbrella term for those neurocognitive processes required to sustain goal-directed problem solving (Welsh & Pennington, 1988) or self-regulation over time toward future goals, typically in a social context (Barkley, 2011b). Problems in EF have been observed in various neurological and psychiatric disorders, particularly adult ADHD (Barkley et al., 2008); they have also been found to be associated with impairment in various major life activities, especially educational and occupational functioning (Barkley & Fischer, 2011; Barkley & Murphy, 2010). EF is believed to be chiefly based upon the functioning of the prefrontal cortex in humans, given that damage in this region has been shown to give rise to substantial disturbances in various EFs (Fuster, 1997; Luria, 1966; Stuss & Benson, 1986).

As noted earlier, participants in the normative sample for the BFIS also completed the BDEFS (Barkley, 2011b). The BDEFS has been shown to assess five interrelated dimensions of EF as described above: Self-Management to Time, Self-Organization/Problem Solving, Self-Discipline, Self-Motivation, and Self-Regulation of Emotions. If deficits in EF are believed to cause impairment in major life activities, then evidence for the validity of the BFIS would be apparent in significant relationships between scores on the BDEFS and the BFIS. For this manual, these relationships were examined via Pearson correlations. The results appear in Table 6.3. The relationships for the specific BFIS domain of daily responsibilities have been discussed above. The BDEFS subscales also correlated significantly with all other BFIS domain ratings and with all four BFIS summary scores. Overall, BDEFS ratings shared from 9% to 40% of the variance in impairment ratings across the 15 BFIS domains and with the BFIS summary scores. Thus greater difficulties with EF in daily life activities are associated with greater ratings of impairment on the BFIS.

The relationship between neuropsychological tests of EF and impairment ratings is a different matter. Such tests of EF share little or no variance (<10%) with ratings of EF (Alderman, Burgess, Knight, & Henman, 2003; Barkley & Fischer, 2011; Barkley & Murphy, in press; Bogod, Mateer, & MacDonald, 2003; Burgess, Alderman, Evans, Emslie, & Wilson, 1998; Chaytor, Schmitter-Edgecombe, & Burr, 2006; Hummer et al., 2011; Ready, Stierman, & Paulsen, 2001; Wood & Liossi, 2006). This has led to the conclusion that the two sets of measures are not assessing the same construct. Although no neuropsychological tests of EF were administered to the

TABLE 6.3. Correlations of BFIS Domain and Summary Scores with Ratings from the BDEFS for the Normative Sample

	BDEFS subscales				
BFIS domains	SMT	SOP	SD	SM	SRE
Home–family	.43	.44	.46	.49	42
Home–chores	.44	.56	.39	.43	.46
Work	.50	.52	.43	.45	.55
Social–strangers	.49	.42	.44	.47	.41
Social–friends	.48	.42	.43	.45	.45
Community activities	.49	.44	.42	.44	.44
Education	.57	.55	.48	.47	.56
Marriage/cohabiting/dating	.45	.47	.45	.47	.44
Money management	.35	.44	.39	.38	.39
Driving	.35	.31	.37	.33	.39
Sexual relations	.41	.36	.34	.38	.33
Daily responsibilities	.53	.62	.45	.47	.52
Self-care routines	.37	.40	.31	.34	.40
Health maintenance	.41	.47	.36	.38	.40
Childrearing	.42	.39	.39	.44	.41
Mean Impairment Score (BFIS-LF)	.56	.58	.51	.53	.54
Percent Domains Impaired (BFIS-LF)	.49	.52	.44	.46	.48
Mean Impairment Score (BFIS Quick Screen)	.53	.57	.49	.52	.54
Percent Domains Impaired (BFIS Quick Screen)	.44	.48	.42	.45	.47

Note. SMT, Self-Management to Time; SOP, Self-Organization/Problem Solving; SD, Self-Discipline; SM, Self-Motivation; and SRE, Self-Regulation of Emotion. Analyses are Pearson product–moment correlations. All correlations were significant at $p \leq .001$.

normative sample, past research using both the UMASS and Milwaukee Studies' datasets has found little relationship between tests of EF and global or specific measures of impairment as indexed by the IRS or by other measures of impairment, some of which (e.g., work disability status and employer-related workplace functioning) were discussed earlier in this chapter (Barkley & Fischer, 2011; Barkley & Murphy, in press). This is evident in Table 6.4. This table contains information from the UMASS Study of adults with ADHD, analyzed further for inclusion in this manual. The correlations are presented between the EF ratings collected in that study and the self-ratings and other-ratings of impairment on the IRS, along with the EF tests collected in that study and their relationship to the same IRS ratings. Compare the correlations in the upper half of the table with those in the lower half. The relationships between ratings of EF and impairment ratings are four to five times larger and much more uniformly significant than the correlations between tests of EF and those same impairment ratings.

For this manual, the same sorts of relationships were examined in the Milwaukee Study dataset. Table 6.5 shows the relationships of the EF ratings on the BDEFS to the self-ratings and other-ratings of impairment from the IRS for all Milwaukee

TABLE 6.4. Correlations of Ratings of EF and of Neuropsychological Tests of EF with Self-Ratings and Other-Ratings of Impairment on the IRS, from the UMASS Study of Adults with ADHD

EF measure	IRS (self)	IRS (others)
EF ratings (P-BDEFS)		
Self-Management to Time	.83**	.70**
Self-Organization/Problem Solving	.77**	.58**
Self-Discipline (Inhibition)	.86**	.67**
Self-Motivation	.75**	.62**
Self-Activation/Concentration	.83**	.67**
EF tests		
Digit Span Forward (LAMB)	–.16*	–.16
Digit Span Backward (LAMB)	–.13	–.12
Stroop Color–Word Test—Interference	–.19*	–.15
Wisconsin Card Sorting Test—total correct	.10	.07
Conners Continuous Performance Test—Omissions	.19**	.20*
Conners Continuous Performance Test—Commissions	.27**	.31**
Conners Continuous Performance Test—Reaction Time Variability	.22**	.26**
Five-Points Test—Unique Designs	–.22**	–.22*

Note. P-BDEFS, prototype of the BDEFS. Data from Barkley et al. (2008).
*$p \leq .01$; **$p \leq .001$.

TABLE 6.5. Correlations of Ratings of EF and of Neuropsychological Tests of EF with Self-Ratings and Other-Ratings of Impairment on the IRS from the Milwaukee Study of Hyperactive Children in Young Adulthood

EF measure	IRS (self)	IRS (others)
EF ratings (P-BDEFS)		
Self-Management to Time	.62**	.41**
Self-Organization/Problem Solving	.63**	.44**
Self-Discipline (Inhibition)	.68**	.45**
Self-Motivation	.61**	.36**
Self-Activation	.64**	.35**
EF tests		
Digit Span Total Score (WAIS-III)	–.17	–.24**
Simon Game—Longest Correct Sequence	–.25**	–.25**
Five-Points Test—Unique Designs	–.06	–.19*
Stroop Color–Word Test—Interference	–.16	–.07
Tower of London—number correct	–.14	–.06
Tower of London—time to first move	–.12	–.04
Kaufman Hand Movements Test—number correct	–.20*	–.28**

Note. P-BDEFS, prototype of BDEFS; WAIS-III, Wechsler Adult Intelligence Scale—Third Edition. Data from Barkley et al. (2008).
*$p \leq .01$; **$p \leq .001$.

Study participants in the upper half of the table. Contrast these relationships with those in the lower half of the table between the EF tests collected in that study and the self- and other-ratings of impairment on the IRS. The same pattern emerges as for the UMASS Study in Table 6.4: Ratings of impairment are far more strongly associated with ratings of EF deficits in daily life activities than they are with EF tests.

Therefore, whereas ratings of impairment (such as those on the BFIS or IRS) share substantial variance with ratings of EF deficits in daily life activities (such as those on the BDEFS), they have little relationship to specific tests of EF. This is a major problem for neuropsychological tests of EF, which many investigators believe to be the gold standard for assessment of that construct. Clearly, those tests are not a gold standard if predicting impairment is the important issue. To summarize, there is good evidence of criterion validity for ratings of impairment when compared to ratings of EF in daily life activities, but little evidence of such when impairment ratings are compared to EF tests.

Intelligence and Academic Achievement Skills

Criterion validity can also be indexed by demonstrating low relationships between the construct being examined and constructs believed to have little or no relationship to it. One would expect that degree of global impairment might have a low yet significant relationship with tested general intelligence. No measure of IQ was administered to the normative sample. But IQ was tested with subtests of the Shipley Institute of Living Scale in the UMASS Study (see Barkley et al., 2008). The relationships of the global impairment ratings on the IRS to that measure of IQ were –.15 (p = .009, n = 283) for self-rated total impairment and –.08 (p = NS, n = 212) for ratings of impairment provided by others who knew these participants well. Therefore, although the relationship is statistically significant, self-rated global ratings of impairment share just 2.2% of the variance or less with tested intelligence; other-ratings of impairment are not associated with tested intelligence to any significant degree.

Similar results were evident for the relationship of global impairment ratings in the UMASS Study to basic academic achievement skills as measured with the Wide Range Achievement Test 3 (Jastak & Wilkinson, 1993). The relationships of global self-rated impairment to standard scores on this battery were as follows: Reading (r = –.08, p = NS, n = 279); Spelling (r = –.11, p = NS, n = 279); and Arithmetic (r = –.06, p = NS, n = 278). The relationship of the specific rating of educational impairment on the IRS was likewise not related significantly to any of the achievement scales: Reading (r = –.03, p = NS, n = 304); Spelling (r = –.09, p = NS, n = 304); and Arithmetic (r = –.04, p = NS, n = 303). All these nonsignificant relationships suggest that ratings of impairment in major life activities (and those in the educational domain specifically) assess a construct that is largely independent of the constructs assessed by intelligence or academic achievement tests.

Conclusion

Additional research is obviously needed on the reliability, validity, and other psychometric properties of the BFIS. The evidence to date, however, is enough to indicate that it has quite satisfactory validity. It is certainly sufficient to recommend its use for assessing adult patients in clinical practice, for studying impairment in research protocols, and for screening adults for possible psychosocial impairment in industrial/organizational settings. The scores from the BFIS (or its predecessor, the IRS) are significantly related to difficulties in numerous domains of major life activities. These include a greater likelihood of impairment or adversity in education, work, money management, driving, and marriage/cohabiting/dating relationships, among others, as well as symptoms of ADHD in adults and extent of EF deficits in daily life.

CHAPTER 7

Scoring and Interpretation of the BFIS Forms

The BFIS can be used to obtain self- and other-ratings of impairment in 15 major life activity domains in adults ages 18–89 years. This can be done quickly and inexpensively in a clinical practice, research setting, or industrial/organizational setting, among others. The BFIS is intended to be used by trained professionals in clinical, research, or industrial/organizational specialties who have sufficient educational background and experience in the evaluation of human psychological functioning and psychosocial impairment. Interpreting the BFIS scales, scores, and profiles requires graduate training in a psychological, psychiatric, or medical specialty at an accredited college or university; in particular, it requires training and coursework in the administration and interpretation of psychological measures. Besides carefully reviewing and understanding this manual, examiners using the BFIS should be familiar with the *Standards for Educational and Psychological Testing* (American Educational Research Association, American Psychological Association, & National Council on Measurement in Education, 1999).

BFIS Materials

The BFIS-LF is likely to yield more reliable information about the extent of general (pervasive) psychosocial impairment because of the greater number of domains it contains. But where time is of the essence, the BFIS Quick Screen can be used as a means of rapidly identifying the likelihood that an individual is impaired in major life activities because it covers the six domains most often screened in clinical evaluations, disability/Social Security examinations, or other determinations in which impairment is being assessed. When clinically significant problems are evident, then a follow-up evaluation can be done with the BFIS-LF if the examiner wishes to obtain broader coverage. As many as 17 scores can be obtained from the BFIS-LF: up to 15 specific domain ratings (1 rating for each domain answered by the participant), a Mean Impairment Score, and a Percent Domains Impaired score. As many as 8 scores can be obtained from the BFIS Quick Screen: up to 6 specific domain ratings (1 rating for each domain answered by the participant), a Mean Impairment Score, and a Percent Domains Impaired score. The threshold for defining whether "impairment" exists in any specific domain is the rating equivalent to the 93rd–95th percentile for the *entire* normative sample, not just for that person's specific age grouping. This is also the case for the two summary scores: the Mean Impairment Score and the Percent Domains Impaired score. The threshold and subsequent range of scores constituting this impairment zone and used for making this determination for each domain and summary score are indicated on the score sheets in enlarged **boldface** type.

Why isn't the threshold for impairment determined in relation to the person's age group? It can be, but that becomes problematic for several reasons. First, administrative and legal rulings in the area of disability/impairment determination have stipulated that the standard of comparison for specifying whether someone is impaired is the average person or normal human, not the average person of some specific age group (see Chapter 1). Second, a moment's reflection will show why this must be the case. If impairment is determined only in relation to your age group, and you are an especially elderly person (in your 80s or above), then you may be found to be functioning only slightly worse than others in that age group—say, in driving, self-care routines, or money management. But in fact, relative to the entire population, your functioning in that domain may be substantially worse and may well place you in the impaired range (again, for the BFIS, this is the 93rd–95th percentile or above). If the comparison is not with the entire adult sample, the impairment will not be detected. Your driving may be only slightly worse than that of the average 90-year-old, for instance, but it may be markedly worse than that of the average adult and thus may be impaired—perhaps even enough to warrant discontinuation of your driving privileges.

The BFIS score sheets are constructed so that an examiner can actually make both determinations: impairment relative to the entire normative population (18–89 years), and impairment relative to a person's specific age grouping (18–39, 40–59, 60–89). The percentiles for the raw scores on the score sheet are the percentiles for the person's age group. But the enlarged **boldface** numbers in each row (for each score) indicate the impairment range for the entire normative sample. This allows the examiner to see immediately on the score sheet both whether the person being evaluated has a score at the 93rd–95th percentile for his/her age group *and* whether that person also surpasses that threshold for the entire normative sample (the **boldface** numbers). The reason why the 93rd–95th percentile is specified, rather than just the 93rd, is the 0–9 scoring range used for any specific domain. For example, in the normative sample, a score of 5 may place a person at the 90th percentile, while the next higher score of 6 is equivalent to the 95th percentile. There is no raw score equivalent to the 93rd percentile because there is no score between 5 and 6. Hence the score selected to mark the threshold for determining impairment is the whole-numbered score closest to the 93rd–95th percentile for the entire normative sample.

Two versions of the BFIS-LF are provided in the Appendix: a Self-Report form and an Other-Report form. Norms (percentiles) are only available for the Self-Report version. The Other-Report version is to be collected and scored for comparison to the Self-Report scores, so as to evaluate the degree of disparity between the index person's self-ratings and those of someone who knows the person well. Large disparities should be explored for their possible reasons in a follow-up clinical interview with the index person and, if available, the collateral adult.

A follow-up interview can be conducted with the assistance of the BFIS Impairment Interview form if a person rates him-/herself (or someone else rates him/her) at or above the 93rd percentile, either relative to the person's specific age group or (especially) relative to the normative population. The Impairment Interview Form is simply a form that lists the 15 specific domains of major life activity from the BFIS, with space underneath each domain for clinical notes. This form is used to obtain specific information from the index person (or the significant other) as to the basis for the individual's rating in any domain. For instance, imagine that a patient named Jim has provided ratings in the domains of education and driving that place him above the 93rd percentile for the entire normative sample. Before accepting this as prima facie evidence of Jim's impairment in those domains, however, the clinician needs to determine more about the veracity of each rating. On what evidence was it based?

If Jim indicates that he was retained in grade, had trouble completing high school, perhaps needed to get a general equivalency diploma, or had marked problems with taking any timed examination, then this would be relatively credible evidence of impairment in education. The evidence would be especially compelling if Jim's school records corroborated these claims. And when Jim is questioned about the basis for his rating of impairment in the driving domain, if he replies in the interview that he has had his license suspended three times, has had more than 15 speeding tickets in the past 10 years, and has been remanded to driver retraining at least twice, then this evidence certainly enhances the credibility of his self-rating.

Now let's suppose that during the interview, Jim reports that his rating of educational problems is based on the fact that he obtained D's in biochemistry in medical school. However, he has graduated from high school and college, has required no accommodations in any form during his education, is nearing completion of his second year in medical school, and is about to take the U.S. Medical Licensing Examination. Jim explains that he believes he has not done as well as other students in his biochemistry class, and that this is the basis for his rating in the education domain on the BFIS. By no stretch of the imagination should this report be considered as indicating "impairment." Relative to the average person or normal human, this is not credible evidence of significant difficulty functioning effectively in a major life activity. A biochemistry class in a medical school is not a "major" human life activity, no matter how important it may seem to the student at the time. Likewise, suppose Jim explains that his rating of his driving is based on the fact that his spouse or partner constantly nags him about waiting too long before braking to a stop, or that he typically drives 5–10 miles per hour over the posted speed limit on highways. He otherwise has a clean driving record (free of any citations, crashes, license suspensions/revocations, etc.), or he has just a single warning ticket for driving over the speed limit or for double-parking in a city. This would not be considered solid evidence of impaired driving performance by any reasonable clinician.

Notice particularly that the BFIS should not be used as the *sole* determinant of degree of actual impairment. It serves as one source (albeit an important one) of information in making such a determination, but that source must always be "triangulated" against other sources in order for the clinician to make a reasonable determination or judgment of impairment. As noted in Chapter 1, these other sources include (1) the reports of others who know the index person well; (2) the history given by the person upon subsequent interviewing; and (3) the archival records that may be available for a specific domain (school records, driving records, criminal records, work history, military records, medical records, etc.), known as "the paper trail" of impairment. Comparing at least three of these sources should give the clinician a reasonable basis for making a determination of actual impairment in any particular domain.

The BFIS-LF Self-Report version has three score sheets, one for each of three age groups (ages 18–39, 40–59, and 60–89). Normative information is not broken down by sex, given that there were no important sex differences on any of the domain scores or summary scores. Norms and score sheets are not available as yet for individuals older than 89.

Two versions of the BFIS Quick Screen are also provided in the Appendix: again, a Self-Report form and an Other-Report form. As with the BFIS-LF, norms are only available for the Self-Report form. A single score sheet, with a table for each age group, is provided for this version of the Quick Screen. The Other-Report form is to be evaluated in comparison to the Self-Report form to determine possible areas of substantial disparity between the index person's reports and those of another adult who knows him/her. When such disparities are large, the examiner should evaluate their possible basis through a clinical interview with the individuals completing these forms, as discussed above.

For convenience, all versions of the BFIS and all of the score sheets may be photocopied by purchasers of this manual for use in their clinical practice or in their employment setting under the limited reproduction license granted by the publisher (see the front matter of the book for this limited permission).

Appropriate Purposes and Populations for the BFIS

The BFIS forms are not intended to replicate or replace the use of other medical, psychological, and psychiatric methods of evaluation and diagnosis in the determination of psychosocial impairment. They provide information that may be important for the ultimate determination of impairment, but, again, they should never serve as the sole source for such a determination. The BFIS is intended to be used for the evaluation of individuals 18–89 years of age, both men and women. Typically, these will be individuals who reside in the United States, as this country is the source for the normative sample. Use of the BFIS with populations, countries, cultures, or ethnic groups outside the United States may be inappropriate, to the extent that such groups vary from the normative reference sample described in this manual.

Administration

The BFIS-LF or BFIS Quick Screen should be given directly to the person being asked to complete the rating (the index person or a significant other), along with a clear explanation of the purpose for which the rating is being obtained. The examiner should also provide a clear understanding of the instructions for completing the rating scale (see the instructions on the forms in the Appendix), as well as an opportunity to express concerns or ask questions about the scale. For greater efficiency in the evaluation process, the BFIS may be mailed out to individuals to complete before the day of the intended evaluation of which it is only a part. If so, however, this mailing should be accompanied with a cover letter that provides information concerning the purpose to which the BFIS is being put and instructions for its completion. This letter should also contain a means by which the rater can contact the examiner concerning any concerns or questions about the scale or its intended purpose.

The BFIS-LF takes an average of 5–7 minutes or less to complete by the average adult in the general population, whereas the BFIS Quick Screen may take only 3–5 minutes to complete. After the form has been completed, the examiner should review the scale for any missed items and then encourage the rater to complete those items, assuming that the item was simply missed and not answered as "does not apply" (indicated by a circle around the number 99 on the scale). The failure to complete more than a few items on the scale is likely to invalidate the resulting scores and make the use of the normative tables on the score sheets inappropriate. If the scale has been returned by mail and there is no further opportunity to complete any missed items, these items should be answered with 99 (does not apply) to create a conservative bias to the scores, so that the determination of impairment is not unduly exaggerated. Even then, the failure to complete more than two of the domains on any version of the scale should be considered sufficient cause to invalidate the scale. Again, this rule does not apply to specific domains that were answered with circles around the number 99 (does not apply); those domains have in fact been completed.

Scoring and Interpreting the BFIS-LF

BFIS-LF: Self-Report

Scoring the BFIS is actually very easy. Follow these procedures to score the BFIS-LF: Self-Report:

- Select the BFIS-LF: Self-Report score sheet for the person's age group (18–39, 40–59, 60–89).

- Transfer the scores from each domain of the BFIS-LF onto the score sheet you have selected. Transfer only the scores circled 0–9 to their respective corresponding rows on the score sheet. Do this by circling the raw score in that row that matches the person's rating for this specific domain. For any domain that the person rated as 99 (does not apply), leave that row blank.

• Now compute the Mean Impairment Score. Do this by summing all of the numbers you circled across all of the rows. Then divide that sum by the number of circles (answers) you used to compute that sum. Do *not* count or include the rows that you left blank. In short, the Mean Impairment Score is the total score across all domains the person rated as applying to him/her (all answers of 0–9), divided by the number of domains thus rated. Domains not answered (left blank) or answered with 99 (does not apply) are not used in this computation.

• In the row on the score sheet marked "Mean Impairment Score," find the number that most closely matches the score you just computed and circle it. If the score you calculated has two decimal places, round up the number in the hundredths place to the next highest tenth if it is a 6 or higher. Round it down if it is a 5 or lower. For instance, a score of 4.27 should be rounded up to 4.3, whereas a score of 4.25 should be rounded down to 4.2.

• Next, compute the Percent Domains Impaired score. To do this, look at the specific domain raw scores you have circled on the score sheet. Now simply count all of those circled numbers that are in enlarged **boldface** type. This number is always a **5** or higher. Take the number of answers you circled that are in **boldface** type, and divide this number by the total number of *specific* domains (rows) that you circled. Ignore any empty rows, and ignore the circle you just placed on the row marked "Mean Impairment Score." You are just counting the number of specific domains answered by the respondent. To reiterate, the Percent Domains Impaired score is the number of **boldface** scores that you circled for the specific domains (not the "Mean Impairment Score" row), divided by the number of specific domains that contain answers (circles). The answer will be the number 1.00 or less. To convert this to a percentage, multiply it by 100.

• In the row on the score sheet marked "Percent Domains Impaired," circle the number (percentage) that matches or is closest to the percentage you have just computed.

• You have now finished scoring the BFIS-LF: Self-Report. You should have a circled answer beside each specific domain (row) that was answered by the respondent. And you should have a circled answer beside each of the two rows marked "Mean Impairment Score" and "Percent Domains Impaired."

To determine how deviant (statistically abnormal or rare) the respondent's answers are, look either at the top or first row on the score sheet, or at the bottom or last row. Each of these rows contains the word **Percentiles**: in boldface type. To the right of this word are the percentiles for this age group from the normative sample that correspond to each of the raw scores you circled on the score sheet. Percentiles through the 84th are shown as ranges (i.e., 1–50, 51–74, 75–84), while the 85th percentile and above are given specifically. So just look at each raw score you circled; then look up or down at the first or last row to find the corresponding percentile (or percentile range) for that raw score. This is the person's percentile in the general population for that answer. The higher the percentile, the more deviant the score is in relation to the normative sample (general population). Since as an examiner you will be primarily interested in how deviant a score is, more precise percentile scores are provided for the 85th–99th+ percentiles. You have now determined the percentile for the patient's scores.

To create a visual profile of the person's total range of impairments (pervasiveness), draw lines on the form that connect the circles starting from the first domain row (home–family) and continuing downward to the last circle. Do not connect the circles in cases where there is a blank row or gap between them. Only draw lines to connect circles that are adjacent to each other.

Remember that you are determining the person's deviance in two ways. First, you can see deviance *relative to the person's age group* by just looking at the percentiles that correspond to the raw answers you circled on this form. Those percentiles are indicated in the top and bottom rows of the table. Next, you can determine deviance *relative to the entire population sample* (ages 18–89) by seeing whether the answer that you circled is in enlarged **boldface** type or not. If it is, then that score is at or above the 93rd to 95th percentile for the population, regardless of what percentile it represents for that specific age group. In short, you can interpret "degree of impairment" both ways: relative to the age group, and relative to the average person in the entire 18- to 89-year-old population.

BFIS-LF: Other-Report

As discussed earlier, the purpose of the Other-Report form of the BFIS-LF is to allow clinicians or researchers to obtain the reports of an adult who knows the index person well enough to complete the BFIS concerning that person. But norms and percentile scores are not available for scoring and interpreting the Other-Report form relative to a general population sample. Instead, you should compare the raw scores obtained on the Self- and Other-Report forms for the degree of their disparity or disagreement. Some such disparity is to be expected, and generally it is greater in the clinic-referred population than in the normal or general population. The greater the disparity, however, the more you will need to inquire in a clinical interview about possible reasons for such wide variation. In doing so, you can at least look at the score sheets to see what percentiles correspond to the Other-Report scores, *as if* they were scores from the Self-Report form. Drastic differences between the percentiles from the two forms will be even further justification for conducting interviews with these individuals.

Research on such self–other rating disparities in regard to adult ADHD has been discussed in Chapter 5 (see "Interobserver Agreement and Disparity"). This research has indicated that spouses/cohabiting partners may be in the best position to provide such reports about current functioning, given the frequency with which they are able to observe the adults being rated (Barkley et al., in press). However, the variation in other-reports as a function of the others' relationship to the index persons is relatively minor. More important appears to be the age of the index persons. Younger individuals, particularly below 27 years of age, often report substantially lower levels of impairment than do those who know them well. In contrast, individuals at least 30 and older appear to report higher levels of impairment than do others who know them well. Our research on the prototype of the BFIS (the IRS) has also shown that the degree of disparity is significantly related to the index persons' degree of ADHD, both in a general population and in clinical samples.

In clinical samples, the index persons' degrees of anxiety and depression are also related to the size of the disparity in IRS ratings. Again, the presence of large self–other disparities on the BFIS should be a signal to explore the presence of these comorbid disorders as a possible explanation for such disparities.

Of course, as discussed in Chapter 1, another explanation for a case in which an index person's ratings are grossly higher than those provided by a significant other may be feigning or malingering. You can further evaluate this possibility by, again, triangulating the self-reported ratings against not only the ratings provided by the other (which can also be feigned if the other is collaborating in the fraud), but also the archival records available for many of the specific BFIS domains. If there is doubt about the credibility of the answers on the Other-Report form, ask to have a copy of this form sent to a third person who does not have the same type of relationship to the respondent as the significant other from whom you already obtained a rating. If that person is a friend or spouse/partner, then ask to have a parent or sibling complete the form, or vice versa.

Scoring the BFIS Quick Screen

Scoring the Self-Report version of the BFIS Quick Screen is obviously easier than scoring the BFIS-LF: Self-Report, but it is still done in essentially the same way:

- Select the score sheet for the BFIS Quick Screen: Self-Report. It contains three tables. Choose the table for the person's age group (18–39, 40–59, 60–89).
- Transfer the scores from each of the six specific domains on the Quick Screen onto the score sheet table for that person's age group. Transfer only the scores circled 0–9 to their respective corresponding rows on the score sheet. Do this by circling the raw score in that row that matches the person's rating for this specific domain. For any domain that the person rated as 99 (does not apply), leave that row blank.
- Now compute the Mean Impairment Score. Do this by summing all of the numbers you circled across all of the rows. Then divide that sum by the number of circles (answers) you used to compute that sum. Do *not* count or include the rows that you left blank. In short, the Mean Impairment Score is the total score across all domains the person rated as applying to him/her (all answers of 0–9), divided by the number of domains thus rated. Domains not answered (left blank) or answered with 99 (does not apply) are not used in this computation.
- In the row on the score sheet table marked "Mean Impairment Score," find the number that most closely matches the score you just computed and circle it. As for the BFIS-LF, if the score you calculated has two decimal places, round up the number in the hundredths place to the next highest tenth if it is a 6 or higher. Round it down if it is a 5 or lower.
- Next, compute the Percent Domains Impaired score. To do this, look at the specific domain raw scores you have circled on the answer sheet. Now simply count all of those circled numbers that are in enlarged **boldface** type. This number is always a **5** or higher. Take the number of answers you circled that are in **boldface**

type, and divide this number by the total number of *specific* domains (rows) that you circled. Ignore any empty rows, and ignore the circle you just placed on the row marked "Mean Impairment Score." You are just counting the number of specific domains answered by the respondent. To reiterate, the Percent Domains Impaired score is the number of **boldface** scores that you circled for the specific domains (not the "Mean Impairment Score" row), divided by the number of specific domains that contain answers (circles). The answer will be the number 1.00 or less. To convert this to a percentage, multiply it by 100.

- In the row on the Score Sheet marked "Percent Domains Impaired," circle the number (percentage) that matches or is closest to the percentage you have just computed.

- You have now finished scoring the BFIS Quick Screen: Self-Report. You should have a circled answer beside each specific domain (row) that was answered by the respondent. And you should have a circled answer beside each of the two rows marked "Mean Impairment Score" and "Percent Domains Impaired."

To determine how deviant (statistically abnormal or rare) the respondent's answers are, look either at the top or first row in the table on the score sheet, or at the bottom or last row. Each of these rows contains the word **Percentiles** in boldface type. To the right of this word are the percentiles for this age group from the normative sample that correspond to each of the raw scores you circled on the score sheet. Percentiles through the 84th are shown as ranges (i.e., 1–50, 51–74, 75–84), while the 85th percentile and above are given specifically. So just look at each raw score you circled; then look up or down at the first or last row of the table to find the corresponding percentile for that raw score. This is the person's percentile (or percentile range) in the general population for that answer. The higher the percentile, the more deviant the score is in relation to the normative sample (general population). Since you will be primarily interested in how deviant a score is, more precise percentile scores are provided for the 85th–99th+ percentiles. You have now determined the percentile for the patient's scores.

To create a visual profile of the person's total range of impairments (pervasiveness), draw lines on the form that connect the circles starting from the first domain row (home–family) and continuing downward to the last circle. Do not connect the circles in cases where there is a blank row or gap between them. Only draw lines to connect circles that are adjacent to each other.

The raw scores on the Other-Report form for the BFIS Quick Screen can be compared to those from the Self-Report form, as described earlier for the BFIS-LF. Once again, sizeable disparities should be a cause for further evaluation of their basis through a clinical interview with the index person and, if possible, with the person who completed the Other-Report form. As noted above, evidence suggests that the severity of ADHD, anxiety, and depression can contribute to such greater-than-typical disparities, and the possible presence of these disorders should be explored further in the clinical evaluation. No data on the BFIS Quick Screen are available, however, to provide any guidelines for how large a disparity should be considered to be unusual or atypical in the general population. Yet, as with the

BFIS-LF, you can at least look at the score sheet for the BFIS Quick Screen: Self-Report to see what the equivalent percentiles would be for the various raw scores from the Other-Report form. In other words, you can look up the percentiles for the Other-Report raw scores *as if* they were raw scores from the Self-Report form. You can then determine whether those percentiles differ vastly from the ones obtained for the Self-Report form. Dramatic differences between the actual percentiles from the Self-Report form and those obtained from this hypothetical inspection of the norms with the Other-Report form would constitute a good reason for clinical interviewing of these individuals.

Again, any answer placing at the 93rd–95th percentile or higher is clinically significant and may indicate the possibility of actual impairment. Once more, scores on these rating scales should not be used alone to render a determination of actual impairment in an adult, but only to indicate a heightened risk for such impairment. The actual impairment must be confirmed by a more thorough clinical evaluation in which sources of information are triangulated against each other, as recommended in Chapter 1 and earlier in this chapter.

Using the BFIS to Evaluate Response to Treatment

The BFIS-LF can be a valuable tool in evaluating an individual's response to treatment, such as physical rehabilitation after medical disorders or injuries, cognitive training as part of neurorehabilitation interventions, cognitive-behavioral treatment of adults with mental disorders, or medication regimens. Both the Self-Report and Other-Report forms can be used for this purpose. The BFIS Quick Screen (both forms) can also be used for this purpose and is even less time-consuming and more cost-effective; its drawback, however, is that it only samples 6 domains of major life activity. The BFIS-LF is not overly cumbersome and takes just a few minutes more to complete than the Quick Screen, while assessing a wider range (15) of major life activity domains.

Various methods exist for determining how much change should be considered a positive (or negative) response to treatment. The choice is often arbitrary, such as a change of 20%, 30%, or 40% from the baseline score. But several statistical approaches are better for this purpose because, unlike such arbitrarily defined thresholds for change, these approaches take into consideration the test–retest reliability of the measure and the variation in change scores in the samples (or general population). One commonly used method is the "reliable change index" (RCI) developed initially by Jacobson and Truax (1991; see also Jacobson, Roberts, Berns, & McGlinchey, 1999). Calculating the RCI helps to determine whether the degree of change in a score is due to chance alone 5% or less of the time. In other words, the examiner can have confidence that such a change score is not due to unreliability, measurement error, or typical variation within a sample.

An RCI is calculated as follows: $(\chi_1 - \chi_2)/S_{\text{diff}}$, where χ_1 is the individual's pretest score and χ_2 is the posttest score. The difference between the two is then divided by the standard error of the difference scores (S_{diff}). S_{diff} can be obtained directly from our results by using the standard deviations listed in Table 4.1 and the formula provided in the article by Jacobson and Truax (1991). But to save you time, the RCI values needed to indicate a significant change on the BFIS-LF or BFIS Quick Screen have been computed for your convenience. These RCI values are shown in Table 7.1 for each age group. To use them, simply take the index person's posttest score and subtract it from his/her pretest score. Then look in Table 7.1 under the appropriate column for the person's age group. Look at the row that corresponds to the domain or summary score in which you are interested. If the difference in the pre- to posttest scores is equal to or greater than the number shown in this cell of Table 7.1 for the person's age group and score, then this difference can be considered to be reliable, or outside the measure's range of error. Probably the best score to use in these cases would be the Mean Impairment Score, but the individual domain scores of the BFIS can also be examined for their reliable change if that is of interest.

A change in scores may be reliable, but that does not necessarily make it clinically significant or meaningful. Clinical significance can be determined by assessing whether the person's score after treatment now falls within the "normal" range of scores. For this determination, Jacobson and Truax (1991) have recommended that the posttreatment score should now place within 2 *SD*s of the mean, or the 98th percentile, for the normal population. This is a fairly generous interpretation

TABLE 7.1. The Reliable Change Index (RCI) Necessary for Pre- to Posttreatment Difference Scores to Be Significant (Reliable) on the BFIS-LF and BFIS Quick Screen

	RCI by age group		
Score	18–39	40–59	60–89
Home–family	4.42	4.02	3.65
Home–chores	4.99	4.80	4.22
Work	3.72	3.72	2.91
Social–strangers	3.37	2.93	3.37
Social–friends	3.43	3.13	2.09
Community activities	4.51	4.51	3.92
Education	6.01	5.15	4.72
Marriage/cohabiting/dating	4.08	3.92	3.14
Money management	5.45	4.84	3.83
Driving	3.13	2.69	1.94
Sexual relations	5.30	5.50	5.30
Daily responsibilities	4.70	4.51	3.38
Self-care routines	4.75	4.35	3.36
Health maintenance	5.54	5.32	4.26
Childrearing	4.21	3.33	3.68
Mean Impairment Score (BFIS-LF)	2.93	2.79	2.35
Percent Domains Impaired (BFIS-LF)	42.9	40.1	30.2
Mean Impairment Score (BFIS Quick Screen)	2.98	2.84	2.39
Percent Domains Impaired (BFIS Quick Screen)	47.3	44.5	33.6

of "normalization." Others might recommend that the posttreatment score should place within 1.5 *SD*s of the normal mean, or approximately the 93rd percentile, since that is a threshold often used to determine whether someone is clinically impaired or not. These demarcations for the general population sample for each age group are provided in Table 7.2. Thus, (1) if a person has shown a change in scores from pre- to posttreatment that meets or surpasses the RCI score in Table 7.1, *and* (2) if the person's posttreatment score is within 1.5 or 2 *SD*s of the mean for the normative sample (depending on how lenient the chosen definition of recovery is), then one could conclude that the treatment has resulted not only in reliable change but also in recovery or normalization.

As an example, let us consider a female patient with adult ADHD who is 35 years of age and manifesting significant impairment in her daily life, as reflected in a BFIS-LF Mean Impairment Score of 7.0. According to the appropriate BFIS-LF: Self-Report score sheet in the Appendix for this patient, she is at the 98th percen-

TABLE 7.2. Thresholds for Determining Normalization or Recovery at Posttreatment Testing

	Age group					
	18–39		40–59		60–89	
Score	1.5	2.0	1.5	2.0	1.5	2.0
Home–family	5.5	6.7	5.1	6.2	4.4	5.4
Home–chores	6.9	8.2	6.7	8.0	5.5	6.6
Work	5.7	6.9	5.4	6.6	4.4	5.3
Social–strangers	5.8	7.0	4.8	5.8	5.7	6.9
Social–friends	5.5	6.7	5.1	6.2	4.4	4.8
Community activities	5.6	6.8	5.6	6.8	4.6	5.6
Education	6.9	8.3	5.6	6.8	5.1	6.2
Marriage/cohabiting/dating	6.6	7.9	6.1	7.4	4.6	5.6
Money management	6.6	8.0	5.9	7.1	4.7	5.2
Driving	4.5	5.6	4.4	4.8	2.7	3.4
Sexual relations	6.2	7.5	6.6	8.0	6.2	7.5
Daily responsibilities	6.2	7.5	5.9	7.1	4.8	5.2
Self-care routines	5.2	6.4	4.8	5.9	3.5	4.4
Health maintenance	6.6	7.9	6.4	7.7	4.6	5.6
Childrearing	5.5	6.7	4.4	5.4	4.5	5.6
Mean Impairment Score (BFIS-LF)	5.1	6.1	4.9	5.8	3.8	4.6
Percent Domains Impaired (BFIS-LF)	47.5	58.7	43.9	54.5	30.2	38.2
Mean Impairment Score (BFIS Quick Screen)	5.3	6.3	5.0	6.0	4.0	4.8
Percent Domains Impaired (BFIS Quick Screen)	50.4	62.9	47.2	58.9	32.8	41.7

Note. Thresholds are provided for +1.5 (93rd percentile) and +2 *SD*s (98th%) above the mean of the normative sample for each age group for scores on the BFIS-LF and BFIS Quick Screen.

tile of the normative population of 18- to 39-year-olds. Following the introduction of treatment for a month with an ADHD medication, the individual completes the BFIS-LF again and now has a Mean Impairment Score of 3.6. According to the same score sheet in the Appendix, the patient now places within the 75th–84th percentile range. Is this degree of change from the medication treatment reliable? That is, is it likely to fall outside the realm of measurement error or unreliability? To find out, let us compute the patient's change score as follows: pretest score (7.0) minus posttest score (3.6) = 3.4 points. Table 7.1 shows that for 18- to 39-year-olds, an RCI of 2.93 is needed for the change in the Mean Impairment Score to be considered reliable. The patient's change score of 3.4 points clearly exceeds that threshold and thus can be considered reliable. Thus the clinician can feel confident that the improvement in mean or average impairment is not simply due to measurement error or unreliability and is likely to be a consequence of the treatment. The patient can be considered a treatment responder in this instance (assuming that side effects of the medication are not so annoying as to warrant treatment discontinuation).

Next we wish to know whether this patient has been "normalized" by the treatment—that is, whether the intervention has brought her to within the normal range. Table 7.2 shows that the threshold for 2 *SD*s above the normal mean for 18- to 39-year-olds is 6.1, which corresponds to approximately the 98th percentile. The patient's posttest score of 3.6 is well below this figure and so can be considered to place within the broadly defined normal range. As noted above, however, some clinicians and researchers believe that this is too generous a definition of "normalization" for determining recovery. Using the criterion of 1.5 *SD*s above the normal mean may be preferred. In that case, the appropriate column of Table 7.2 indicates that this threshold is 5.1. The patient's posttest score of 3.6 is also below this level. Even by this more conservative definition of "normalization," the patient still can be considered to place within the broadly defined normal range for her age group. This may be considered "recovery." In fact, according to the means and *SD*s in Table 4.1 for the 18–39 age group, this patient's score is less than 1 *SD* above the normal mean ($M = 2.3$, $SD = 1.9$). According to this empirical RCI-based approach to defining "treatment response" and "normalization," the treatment has been successful.

Of course, ADHD medications may provide only symptomatic relief in such cases, and only when the medication is taken at therapeutic levels. The terms "reliable change" (or "treatment response") and "normalization" therefore refer here only to a temporary effect of the medication while in use, and not to a permanent alteration of the patient's functioning in the absence of medication management. It will also be clinically informative to have someone who knows the patient well complete the same version of the BFIS before and after treatment as a check on the validity of the patient's reports. In conducting medication studies of adults with ADHD, I have found that others who know the patients well may actually detect changes in the patients' functioning earlier than, at lower doses than, or to a greater extent than the patients do in their self-reports. It should become standard practice to compare patients' self-reports with the reports of collateral adults who know the patients well. This should be done both to establish pretreatment status and to determine changes that may be occurring as a function of treatment.

Evaluating Increase in Impairment Due to Brain Injury

A very similar approach can be taken to evaluating whether or not an individual has experienced a significant deterioration in adaptive functioning following some form of brain injury—whether the origin is a traumatic, infectious, cancerous, or vascular event, or some other causal factor (e.g., open-heart surgery, cancer treatments such as radiation or chemotherapy, or a hypoxic episode such as near-drowning). A clinician here may be asking this question: Has a reliable and significant increase in impairment occurred in this patient? The RCI figures in Table 7.1 can be used as a crude guideline to determine whether the deterioration in functioning is reliable (i.e., probably outside the realm of measurement error). The patient (let us assume this time that the patient is a man) can complete the Self-Report form of either the BFIS-LF or the BFIS Quick Screen on how he believes he is functioning now. He can then complete a second version with reference to how well he believes he was functioning prior to the event. This assumes, naturally, that memory for premorbid functioning is not believed to have been adversely affected by this event. To increase clinical confidence on the matter, the clinician should have someone who knows this patient well complete the Other-Report form for the same version of the BFIS, concerning both the patient's premorbid status and his postmorbid functioning. Then the clinician can compare the patient's pre- and postmorbid Mean Impairment Scores on both the Self- and Other-Reports.

Once again, to get the RCI, subtract the postmorbid from the premorbid score; in this case, the result will be negative. Now look in Table 7.1 for the Mean Impairment Score for the patient's age group. If the change in the patient's scores is equal to or greater than the RCI value given in the table, the patient's deterioration in functioning can be considered reliable; that is, the change is probably outside the realm of measurement error or unreliability. The thresholds provided in Table 7.2 for the patient's age group and BFIS scores can now be used to determine whether this patient's scores place him outside the normal range; both the 1.5-*SD* and 2-*SD* thresholds (approximately the 93rd and 98th percentiles) can be used. This will enable the clinician to say that the patient's postmorbid score is now more likely to have been drawn from a distribution of individuals with significant impairment in daily life activities than to have been drawn from the general adult population.

Once again, it will prove clinically useful to do the same comparisons for the Other-Report forms completed by someone who knows this patient well, to see whether similar changes are being reported in the pre- to postmorbid BFIS scores. The entries in Tables 7.1 and 7.2 are based only on the Self-Report versions of the BFIS. Even so, one can still use the Other-Report forms to provide some further information about the changes being seen in such a case—that is, as a check on the validity of the patient's self-reports.

In the present example, the clinician may find that the patient has substantially underreported the increase that occurred in his impairment as a consequence of the brain injury, relative to the reports of someone who knows him well. This may be because the patient's self-awareness has been so dramatically compromised by the injury that he cannot be considered a valid reporter of his own postmorbid status. Given that self-awareness is a major component of EF, and that EF is mediated largely by the prefrontal cortex, such an underreporting of change in self-ratings may well be a consequence of an injury to this part of the brain.

Interpreting the BFIS

A competent professional interpretation of BFIS results begins with a thorough understanding of the nature of psychosocial impairment and of the disorders that may be contributing to it. Chapter 1 can serve as an introduction to the topic of psychosocial impairment. But it is not a substitute for a thorough grounding in the larger scientific and clinical literature on impairment determination (see, e.g., Goldstein & Naglieri, 2009), especially if an examiner is making disability, Social Security, Department of Veterans Affairs, or workers' compensation determinations. In brief, the BFIS is intended to measure a person's degree of self-reported impairment in major domains of daily life activities. Interpretation can be based on the following approaches to understanding the meaning of BFIS scores.

Face Validity

The face validity approach to interpretation is aided by a complete familiarity with the domains included in the scale. A high score on a domain (typically at or above the 93rd percentile, and especially at or above the 98th) may signal an abnormality in this domain of daily life activities. One initial means of interpreting each domain in a clinical report is on the basis of the face validity of that domain. The examiner can actually select the domains a respondent has answered with a response that occurs in **boldface** type on the score sheet for his/her age group and directly interpret this score as an abnormality based on self-report. However, given that the domains are moderately to highly intercorrelated, it is quite likely that an individual will produce deviant scores on more than just one or two domains of the BFIS. It is not an impossible occurrence for a single domain to be clinically elevated, but such an occurrence would be cause for further exploration of the reason for such an unusual event. One possibility may be malingering (see below and Chapter 1). Also in view of this interrelatedness of the domains, computing interdomain differences is not encouraged, as the clinical meaning of such disparities has not been explored in any research to date. This does not mean, however, that relative fluctuations across the domains will not be evident—only that interpreting the meaning of large disparities among them has little empirical basis at this time. Just interpreting the meaning of each domain separately is likely to be sufficient to convey the meaning of the BFIS scores, rather than trying to gain more information from the scale than current research allows.

Normative Comparisons

Interpretation of each BFIS score continues with the comparison of the individual's score to that of the normative population, using the percentiles given on the score sheets in the Appendix. A percentile score represents the person's relative position in comparison to the general population of adults, and specifically to the person's age group. In other words, when the percentile score is used, the individual is said to place at or above this percentage of individuals in the general population of his/her age group in degree of self-rated impairment in daily life activities.

Self–Other Comparisons

Once again, an examiner is strongly encouraged to have someone who knows the participant well complete an Other-Report form, so as to obtain information on interobserver agreement and a quick check on the likely validity of the self-ratings. One reason is that some conditions or disorders (e.g., brain injuries, as discussed above) can result in underreporting of the severity of impairment. Another is that the reports of others can help to evaluate potential malingering in cases in which an individual may immediately gain in some way, such as a financial settlement, criminal sentencing, or access to accommodations in educational or occupational settings under the ADA. Getting such reports from others is not a foolproof method of detecting malingering (the other person may be colluding with the examinee to help him/her obtain such benefits), but doing so clearly increases the probability of detecting it. A further means of detection is to triangulate the results from these two sources of information against other sources, such as archival records of major domains of life activities (educational transcripts, medical records, psychiatric records, employment histories, criminal records, driving records, etc.). Even in the absence of such a "paper trail" of impairment, the clinician can judge the likelihood that significant impairment is present by the person's history of functioning in that major life domain. Here the clinician is evaluating the consistency of the history against the complaints of impairment, as yet another check on the veracity of the impairment rating. It is certainly possible for individuals to feign ratings of impairment on rating scales and even lab tests presumed to evaluate various neuropsychological abilities. Detecting such instances of malingering is not easy, but it can be aided by using certain symptom validity tests designed to catch malingering or symptom exaggeration (Frazier, Frazier, Busch, Kerwood, & Demaree, 2008; Sollman, Ranseen, & Berry, 2010; Suhr, Hammers, Dobbins-Buckland, Zimak, & Hughes, 2008; Sullivan, May, & Galbally, 2007). This is yet another source of information to be considered in the triangulation process (Booksh et al., 2010).

Interpretation of the BFIS can then continue with a discussion of the results of the comparison between self- and other-ratings. A clinician must remember that some disparity is commonplace. Moreover, the clinician must take care not to assume automatically that the ratings on the Other-Report form are somehow more valid than, or should serve as the standard of "truth" for, the participant's self-ratings. This is a relative comparison between two observers, neither of whom has an exclusive claim to the truth. Yet the comparison itself is informative in showing whether one party reports a substantially higher or lower level of impairment than the other does. Also, recall from earlier discussions that certain psychiatric disorders or psychological problems, such as ADHD, anxiety, and depression, have been found to be associated with greater disparities in self–other ratings and should be explored further in the clinical evaluation. This is especially so for anxiety and depression in clinic-referred populations; in the general population, ADHD is a principal correlate of such disparities.

Risk Analysis (Using the Evidence on Criterion Validity)

As discussed in Chapter 6, high scores on the BFIS domains were associated in our research with various difficulties in various areas of major life activities. Therefore, the higher the scores observed on the BFIS, the more likely a participant is to be at risk for problems in these same areas of life activities. These risks should be noted in the clinical interpretation of the larger meaning of the BFIS scores. Difficulties with educational and occupational functioning, marital or cohabiting satisfaction, income and financial management, adverse driving outcomes, and adverse health outcomes, among others, are all correlates of higher BFIS scores that deserve notice by the examiner and probably should be conveyed to the participant whenever appropriate and applicable. Such information can also be linked to what is already known about the participant from the larger clinical evaluation, in which the BFIS should serve as simply one component. The examiner will have information on the individual's history with regard to these and other major domains of life activity, and the BFIS findings can be placed in this larger context. Risk analysis concerning impairments can be further aided by using the BDEFS (Barkley, 2011b), on which national norms are available for self-ratings of potential problems in five dimensions of EF deficits in daily life activities: Self-Management to Time, Self-Organization/ Problem Solving, Self-Discipline, Self-Motivation, and Self-Regulation of Emotion. The BDEFS also has an Other-Report form, which can contribute further to the evaluation of impairment risk in the patient.

Pre- to Postinjury Status

As already noted above, another approach to interpreting the BFIS exists when the scale has been used to assess possible changes in an individual after a neurological injury, or in conjunction with the onset of an acute adverse psychiatric or psychological event. If the BFIS is given twice to an individual (and to a significant other) with instructions to complete one version for preinjury status and the other for postinjury, then these comparisons can be interpreted (with appropriate caution) for the information they may provide about the event's impact on impairment in daily life activities.

Pre- to Posttreatment Change

As discussed above, examiners can also use the BFIS to evaluate possible response to intervention by giving the scale before and after an intervention has been implemented. Guidelines are given above and in Tables 7.1 and 7.2 for how to interpret a change in scores as reflecting (1) reliable change and (2) recovery or normalization. This information can be included in the interpretation of the meaning of the BFIS scores so obtained.

Conclusion

The BFIS provides a clinically informative means of evaluating psychosocial impairment as reported by adults ages 18–89 years and by others who know them well (on its Self-Report and Other-Report forms, respectively). Both a long form (the 15-domain BFIS-LF) and a shorter version (the 6-domain BFIS Quick Screen) can serve to evaluate impairment in daily life activities along specific interrelated dimensions, as well as more global summary scores reflecting mean impairment and percentage of domains impaired. Further research on and clinical experience with the BFIS are strongly encouraged. Meanwhile, substantial evidence obtained to date shows the BFIS to be reasonably reliable, valid, and useful in assessing these 15 dimensions of psychosocial impairment in daily life activities. It is efficient and cost-effective, while also yielding valuable information on the potential risks that such impairment may pose. The adaptive significance of the BFIS is documented in its association with impairment in various domains of major adult life activities. The scale can be used in clinical practice, research, industrial/organizational settings, or any other venues where the evaluation of potential deficits in daily life activities is of interest. It can also serve as a basis for evaluating change in such psychosocial impairment, whether as a consequence of treatment or secondary to the occurrence of various neurological and psychiatric disorders or even transient psychological events. I hope that you, my readers, find the BFIS useful in your practice.

APPENDIX

BFIS and Score Sheets

BFIS-LF: Self-Report

Name: ______________________________ Date: ____________________

Sex: (Circle one) Male Female Age: ______________

Instructions

How much difficulty do you have functioning effectively in each of these major life activities? That is, to what degree do you see yourself as being impaired in each of these life domains? Please circle the number next to each item that best describes your difficulties in functioning **DURING THE PAST 6 MONTHS**. If that situation does not apply to you (for instance, you don't drive a car, don't have children, don't live with anyone, etc.), please circle the 99 in the last column (under "Does not apply").

Major Life Activities	Not at all	Somewhat		Mild		Moderate			Severe		Does not apply
1. In your home life with your immediate family	0	1	2	3	4	5	6	7	8	9	99
2. In getting chores completed at home and managing your household	0	1	2	3	4	5	6	7	8	9	99
3. In your work or occupation	0	1	2	3	4	5	6	7	8	9	99
4. In your social interactions with strangers and acquaintances	0	1	2	3	4	5	6	7	8	9	99
5. In your relationships with friends	0	1	2	3	4	5	6	7	8	9	99
6. In your activities in the community (church, clubs, social groups, organizations)	0	1	2	3	4	5	6	7	8	9	99
7. In any educational activities (college, night classes, technical training, occupational training)	0	1	2	3	4	5	6	7	8	9	99
8. In your marital, co-living, or dating relationships	0	1	2	3	4	5	6	7	8	9	99
9. In your management of your money, your bills, and your debts	0	1	2	3	4	5	6	7	8	9	99
10. In driving a motor vehicle and in your history of citations and accidents	0	1	2	3	4	5	6	7	8	9	99

(cont.)

Major Life Activities	Not at all	Somewhat		Mild		Moderate			Severe		Does not apply
11. In your sexual activities and sex relations with others	0	1	2	3	4	5	6	7	8	9	99
12. In your organization and management of your daily responsibilities	0	1	2	3	4	5	6	7	8	9	99
13. In caring for yourself daily (dressing, bathing and hygiene, eating, sleeping, etc.)	0	1	2	3	4	5	6	7	8	9	99
14. In maintaining your health (exercise, nutrition, preventive medical and dental care, etc.)	0	1	2	3	4	5	6	7	8	9	99
15. In taking care of and raising your children	0	1	2	3	4	5	6	7	8	9	99

Office Use Only:

Sum the number of items circled 0 to 9 across all of the domains above, and enter score here: _______. (Do not count answers of 99.)

Divide this sum by the number of circled answers you used to create the sum above (the number of domains the individual rated 0–9). Enter score below:

Mean Impairment Score:______

BFIS Quick Screen: Self-Report

Name: ______________________________ Date: ______________

Sex: (Circle one) Male Female Age: ______________

Instructions

How much difficulty do you have functioning effectively in each of these major life activities? That is, to what degree do you see yourself as being impaired in each of these life domains? Please circle the number next to each item that best describes your difficulties in functioning **DURING THE PAST 6 MONTHS**. If that situation does not apply to you (for instance, you don't drive a car, don't have children, don't live with anyone, etc.), please circle the 99 in the last column (under "Does not apply").

Major Life Activities	Not at all	Somewhat		Mild		Moderate			Severe		Does not apply
1. In your home life with your immediate family	0	1	2	3	4	5	6	7	8	9	99
2. In getting chores completed at home and managing your household	0	1	2	3	4	5	6	7	8	9	99
3. In your work or occupation	0	1	2	3	4	5	6	7	8	9	99
4. In your relationships with friends	0	1	2	3	4	5	6	7	8	9	99
5. In any educational activities (college, night classes, technical training, occupational training)	0	1	2	3	4	5	6	7	8	9	99
6. In caring for yourself daily (dressing, bathing and hygiene, eating, sleeping, etc.)	0	1	2	3	4	5	6	7	8	9	99

Office Use Only:

Sum the number of items circled 0 to 9 across all of the domains above, and enter score here: _______. (Do not count answers of 99.)

Divide this sum by the number of circled answers you used to create the sum above (the number of domains the individual rated 0–9). Enter score below:

Mean Impairment Score: ______

BFIS-LF: Other-Report

Name of person to be rated: ______________________ Date: ______________

Your name: ____

Your relationship to person being rated: (Circle one)

Mother Father Brother/sister Spouse/partner Friend Other (specify): ____________

Instructions

You are being asked to describe the behavior of someone whom you know well. How much difficulty does this person have functioning effectively in each of these major life activities? That is, to what degree is he/she impaired in each of these life domains? Please circle the number next to each item that best describes his/her difficulties in functioning **DURING THE PAST 6 MONTHS**. If that situation does not apply to this person (for instance, he/she doesn't drive a car, doesn't have children, doesn't live with anyone, etc.), please circle the 99 in the last column (under "Does not apply").

Major Life Activities	Not at all	Somewhat		Mild		Moderate			Severe		Does not apply
1. In person's home life with his/her immediate family	0	1	2	3	4	5	6	7	8	9	99
2. In getting chores completed at home and managing his/her household	0	1	2	3	4	5	6	7	8	9	99
3. In his/her work or occupation	0	1	2	3	4	5	6	7	8	9	99
4. In his/her social interactions with strangers and acquaintances	0	1	2	3	4	5	6	7	8	9	99
5. In his/her relationships with friends	0	1	2	3	4	5	6	7	8	9	99
6. In his/her activities in the community (church, clubs, social groups, organizations)	0	1	2	3	4	5	6	7	8	9	99
7. In any educational activities (college, night classes, technical training, occupational training)	0	1	2	3	4	5	6	7	8	9	99
8. In his/her marital, co-living, or dating relationships	0	1	2	3	4	5	6	7	8	9	99

(cont.)

Major Life Activities	Not at all	Somewhat		Mild		Moderate			Severe		Does not apply
9. In his/her management of money, bills, and debts	0	1	2	3	4	5	6	7	8	9	99
10. In driving a motor vehicle and in his/her history of citations and accidents	0	1	2	3	4	5	6	7	8	9	99
11. In his/her sexual activities and sex relations with others	0	1	2	3	4	5	6	7	8	9	99
12. In his/her organization and management of daily responsibilities	0	1	2	3	4	5	6	7	8	9	99
13. In caring for him-/herself daily (dressing, bathing and hygiene, eating, sleeping, etc.)	0	1	2	3	4	5	6	7	8	9	99
14. In maintaining his/her health (exercise, nutrition, preventive medical and dental care, etc.)	0	1	2	3	4	5	6	7	8	9	99
15. In taking care of and raising his/her children	0	1	2	3	4	5	6	7	8	9	99

Office Use Only:

Sum the number of items circled 0 to 9 across all of the domains above, and enter score here: _______. (Do not count answers of 99.)

Divide this sum by the number of circled answers you used to create the sum above (the number of domains the individual rated 0–9). Enter score below:

Mean Impairment Score:______

BFIS Quick Screen: Other-Report

Name of person to be rated: ______________________ Date: ______________

Your name: ____

Your relationship to person being rated: (Circle one)

Mother   Father   Brother/sister   Spouse/partner   Friend   Other (specify): ____________

Instructions

You are being asked to describe the behavior of someone whom you know well. How much difficulty does this person have functioning effectively in each of these major life activities? That is, to what degree is he/she impaired in each of these life domains? Please circle the number next to each item that best describes his/her difficulties in functioning **DURING THE PAST 6 MONTHS**. If that situation does not apply to this person (for instance, he/she doesn't drive a car, doesn't have children, doesn't live with anyone, etc.), please circle the 99 in the last column (under "Does not apply").

Major Life Activities	Not at all	Somewhat		Mild		Moderate			Severe		Does not apply
1. In person's home life with his/her immediate family	0	1	2	3	4	5	6	7	8	9	99
2. In getting chores completed at home and managing his/her household	0	1	2	3	4	5	6	7	8	9	99
3. In his/her work or occupation	0	1	2	3	4	5	6	7	8	9	99
4. In his/her relationships with friends	0	1	2	3	4	5	6	7	8	9	99
5. In any educational activities (college, night classes, technical training, occupational training)	0	1	2	3	4	5	6	7	8	9	99
6. In caring for him-/herself daily (dressing, bathing and hygiene, eating, sleeping, etc.)	0	1	2	3	4	5	6	7	8	9	99

Office Use Only:

Sum the number of items circled 0 to 9 across all of the domains above, and enter score here: _______. (Do not count answers of 99.)

Divide this sum by the number of circled answers you used to create the sum above (the number of domains the individual rated 0–9). Enter score below:

Mean Impairment Score: _______

BFIS Impairment Interview

Name of person being interviewed: ______________________________

Person's sex: (Circle one) Male Female Person's age: ______________

Name of interviewer: ______________________________ Date: __________

Instructions

Use this form as part of a follow-up interview after a BFIS Self-Report form has been completed by the participant, returned, and scored. This form is for gathering additional information about those domains that the person has rated as being impaired (i.e., falling at or above the 93rd percentile). Question the person about the specific reasons for and basis of his/her self-reporting moderate to severe impairment in that specific domain of major life activity. What adverse events or consequences have occurred in this domain that would lead the person to believe that he/she is functioning so ineffectively in the domain? Record the answers below, and then use these responses to further evaluate the credibility, veracity, or inappropriateness of the ratings. A separate copy of this same form can be used for interviewing a significant other who has provided the ratings on a BFIS Other-Report form.

Home–family

Home–chores

Work

(cont.)

Social–strangers

Social–friends

Community activities

Education

Marriage/cohabiting/dating

Money management

(cont.)

Driving

Sexual relations

Daily responsibilities

Self-care routines

Health maintenance

Childrearing

BFIS-LF: Self-Report Score Sheet for Raw Scores (Ages 18–39)

Name: ______________________ Age: ______________ Sex: ________ Date: ____________

Raw Score Percentiles

Percentiles:	1–50	51–75	76–84	85	86	87	88	89	90	91	92	93	94	95	96	97	98	99+
Home–family	0–1	2–3	4	—	—	—	—	**5**	—	—	—	—	**6**	—	—	**7**	—	**8–9**
Home–chores	0–2	3–4	5	—	—	6	—	—	—	—	—	**7**	—	—	—	**8**	**9**	—
Work	0–1	2–3	4	—	—	—	5	—	—	—	—	**6**	—	—	—	**7**	**8**	**9**
Social–strangers	0–1	2–4	—	5	—	—	—	—	**6**	—	—	—	—	**7**	—	**8**	**9**	**9**
Social–friends	0	1–2	3–4	—	—	—	—	—	**5**	—	—	**6**	—	—	—	**7**	**8**	**9**
Community activities	0–1	2	3–4	—	—	—	—	5	—	—	—	**6**	—	—	**7**	—	**8**	**9**
Education	0–1	2–4	5	6	—	—	—	—	—	**7**	—	—	—	**8**	**9**	—	—	—
Marriage/ cohabiting/dating	0–1	2–4	5	—	—	6	—	—	—	—	**7**	—	—	—	—	**8**	**9**	—
Money management	0–1	2–4	5	—	—	—	**6**	—	—	—	—	**7**	—	**8**	**9**	—	—	—
Driving	0	1	2	3	4	—	—	—	—	—	—	—	**5**	**6**	—	—	**7**	**8–9**
Sexual relations	0	1–3	4–5	—	—	—	—	6	—	—	—	—	**7**	—	**8**	**9**	—	—
Daily responsibilities	0–1	2–4	—	5	—	—	—	—	**6**	—	—	—	—	—	**7**	—	**8**	**9**
Self-care routines	0	1	2–4	—	—	—	—	—	5	—	—	**6**	—	—	**7**	—	**8**	**9**
Health maintenance	0–1	2–4	5	—	—	—	—	**6**	—	—	—	—	**7**	—	**8**	**9**	—	—
Childrearing	0	1–2	3–4	—	—	—	—	—	5	—	**6**	—	—	**7**	—	—	**8**	**9**
Mean Impairment Score	0.0–1.9	1.9–3.5	3.6–4.5	4.6	4.8	4.9	—	5.0	5.1	**5.2**	**5.3**	**5.5**	**5.8**	**6.0**	**6.3**	**6.8**	**7.0**	**7.9+**
Percent Domains Impaired	0	7–19	20–30	31	33	36	38	42	47	**48**	**50**	**55**	**58**	**60**	**75**	**86**	**93**	**94**
Percentiles:	1–50	51–75	75–84	85	86	87	88	89	90	91	92	93	94	95	96	97	98	99+

Note. Numbers in **boldface** type in each row (representing a specific domain) indicate the start of the range of impairment for that domain (93rd–95th percentile), compared to the *entire* normative sample. Scores at or above this number are considered "impaired" and contribute to the computation of the Percent Domains Impaired score.

BFIS-LF: Self-Report Score Sheet for Raw Scores (Ages 40–59)

Name: ______________________ Age: ____________ Sex: ________ Date: ________

Raw Score Percentiles

Percentiles:	1–50	51–75	76–84	85	86	87	88	89	90	91	92	93	94	95	96	97	98	99+
Home–family	0	1–2	3–4	—	—	—	—	—	**5**	—	—	—	—	**6**	—	—	**7**	**8–9**
Home–chores	0–1	2–4	5	—	—	—	6	—	—	—	—	**7**	—	—	—	—	**8**	**9**
Work	0	1–2	3–4	—	—	—	5	—	—	—	—	—	**6**	—	**7**	—	**8**	**9**
Social–strangers	0–1	2–3	4	—	—	5	—	—	—	—	—	**6**	—	—	**7**	—	**8**	**9**
Social–friends	0–1	2	3–4	—	—	—	—	—	5	—	—	—	—	—	**6**	—	**7**	**8–9**
Community activities	0–1	2–3	4	—	—	—	—	5	—	—	—	**6**	—	—	**7**	**8**	**9**	—
Education	0	1–3	4	—	—	—	—	5	—	—	—	6	—	—	**7**	**8**	**9**	—
Marriage/cohabiting/dating	0–1	2–3	4	5	—	—	—	—	6	—	—	—	**7**	—	—	**8**	**9**	—
Money management	0–1	2–3	4	—	—	5	—	—	—	**6**	—	—	—	**7**	**8**	**9**	—	—
Driving	0	1	2	—	—	3	—	—	—	4	—	—	**5**	—	—	**6**	**7**	**8–9**
Sexual relations	0–1	2–4	5	—	—	6	—	—	—	**7**	—	—	**8**	**9**	—	—	—	—
Daily responsibilities	0–1	2–3	4	—	—	5	—	—	—	**6**	—	—	—	**7**	—	—	**8**	**9**
Self-care routines	0	1	2–3	4	—	—	—	5	—	—	—	—	—	**6**	—	**7**	**8**	**9**
Health maintenance	0–1	2–3	4–5	—	—	—	—	—	—	**6**	—	—	—	**7**	**8**	**9**	—	—
Childrearing	0	1	2	3	—	—	4	—	—	—	—	5	—	—	—	**6**	**7**	**8–9**
Mean Impairment Score	0.0–1.7	1.8–3.3	3.4–4.4	4.5	4.6	4.7	4.8	4.9	5.0	5.1	**5.2**	**5.3**	**5.8**	**6.0**	**6.1**	**6.4**	**6.5**	**6.8+**
Percent Domains Impaired	0	7–14	15–30	33	36	37	38	40	45	46	**50**	**57**	**60**	**67**	**69**	**73**	**77**	**86+**
Percentiles:	1–50	51–75	75–84	85	86	87	88	89	90	91	92	93	94	95	96	97	98	99+

Note. Numbers in **boldface** type in each row (representing a specific domain) indicate the start of the range of impairment for that domain (93rd–95th percentile), compared to the *entire* normative sample. Scores at or above this number are considered "impaired" and contribute to the computation of the Percent Domains Impaired score.

BFIS-LF: Self-Report Score Sheet for Raw Scores (Ages 60–89)

Name: ______________________ Age: ____________ Sex: ______ Date: ________

Raw Score Percentiles

Percentiles:	1–50	51–75	76–84	85	86	87	88	89	90	91	92	93	94	95	96	97	98	99+
Home–family	0	1	2–3	—	—	—	4	—	—	—	—	**5**	—	—	—	**6**	—	**7–9**
Home–chores	0–1	2	3–4	—	—	5	—	—	—	—	—	—	6	—	—	—	**7**	**8–9**
Work	0	1–2	3	—	—	—	—	—	4	—	—	5	—	—	—	**6**	—	**7–9**
Social–strangers	0	1–2	3	—	—	4	—	—	—	—	—	5	—	—	**6**	—	**7**	**8–9**
Social–friends	0	1	2	—	—	3	—	—	—	4	—	—	5	—	—	**6**	—	**7–9**
Community activities	0	1	2	3	—	—	4	—	—	—	5	—	—	6	—	—	—	7–9
Education	0	1	2–3	4	—	—	—	—	—	5	—	—	6	—	—	**7**	**8**	**9**
Marriage/ cohabiting/dating	0	1	2–3	—	4	—	—	—	—	—	5	—	—	—	—	6	**7**	**8–9**
Money management	0	1	2	—	3	—	—	—	4	—	—	—	5	—	—	**6**	—	**7–9**
Driving	0	—	1	—	—	—	—	—	2	—	—	3	—	4	—	**5**	—	**6–9**
Sexual relations	0	1–2	3–5	—	—	—	—	6	—	—	—	—	**7**	—	—	**8**	**9**	—
Daily responsibilities	0	1	2–3	—	—	—	—	4	—	—	—	5	—	—	—	—	**6**	**7–9**
Self-care routines	0	1	—	—	—	—	2	—	3	4	—	—	—	5	—	**6**	—	**7–9**
Health maintenance	0	1	2–3	—	—	—	4	—	—	—	5	—	—	—	—	**6**	**7**	**8–9**
Childrearing	0	1	2–3	4	—	—	—	—	—	—	5	—	—	—	**6**	—	**7**	**8–9**
Mean Impairment Score	0.0–1.1	1.2–2.1	2.2–2.9	3.1	3.2	3.3	3.4	3.6	3.8	4.1	4.2	4.5	4.7	5.0	**5.2**	**5.3**	**5.6**	**6.5+**
Percent Domains Impaired	0	1–7	8–9	11	13	17	18	20	24	25	29	31	38	42	**45**	**55**	**73**	**75+**
Percentiles:	1–50	51–75	75–84	85	86	87	88	89	90	91	92	93	94	95	96	97	98	99+

Note. Numbers in **boldface** type in each row (representing a specific domain) indicate the start of the range of impairment for that domain (93rd–95th percentile), compared to the *entire* normative sample. Scores at or above this number are considered "impaired" and contribute to the computation of the Percent Domains Impaired score.

BFIS Quick Screen: Self-Report Score Sheet for Raw Scores (All Ages)

Name: ______________________ Age: __________ Sex: ______ Date: ______

Raw Score Percentiles (Ages 18–39)

Percentiles:	1–50	51–75	76–84	85	86	87	88	89	90	91	92	93	94	95	96	97	98	99+
Home–family	0–1	2–3	4	—	—	—	—	**5**	—	—	—	—	**6**	—	—	**7**	—	**8–9**
Home–chores	0–2	3–4	5	—	—	6	—	—	—	—	—	**7**	—	—	—	**8**	**9**	—
Work	0–1	2–3	4	—	—	—	5	—	—	—	—	**6**	—	—	—	**7**	**8**	**9**
Social–friends	0	1–2	3–4	—	—	—	—	—	5	—	—	**6**	—	—	—	**7**	**8**	**9**
Education	0–1	2–4	5	6	—	—	—	—	—	**7**	—	—	—	**8**	**9**	—	—	—
Self-care routines	0	1	2–4	—	—	—	—	—	5	—	—	**6**	—	—	**7**	—	**8**	**9**
Mean Impairment Score	0.0–1.6	1.7–3.6	3.7–4.6	4.7	4.8	4.9	5.0	5.2	5.4	**5.5**	**5.6**	**5.8**	**5.9**	**6.0**	**6.3**	**7.0**	**7.4**	**8.0+**
Percent Domains Impaired	0	17	20–25	26	33	35	40	42	44	46	**50**	**60**	**65**	**80**	**83**	**85**	**87**	**88**
Percentiles:	1–50	51–75	75–84	85	86	87	88	89	90	91	92	93	94	95	96	97	98	99+

Raw Score Percentiles (Ages 40–59)

Percentiles:	1–50	51–75	75–84	85	86	87	88	89	90	91	92	93	94	95	96	97	98	99+
Home–family	0	1–2	3–4	—	—	—	—	—	**5**	—	—	—	—	**6**	—	—	**7**	**8–9**
Home–chores	0–1	2–4	5	—	—	—	6	—	—	—	—	**7**	—	—	—	—	**8**	**9**
Work	0	1–2	3–4	—	—	—	5	—	—	—	—	—	**6**	—	**7**	—	**8**	**9**
Social–friends	0–1	2	3–4	—	—	—	—	—	5	—	—	—	—	—	**6**	—	**7**	**8–9**
Education	0	1–3	4	—	—	—	—	5	—	—	—	6	—	—	**7**	**8**	**9**	—
Self-care routines	0	1	2–3	4	—	—	—	5	—	—	—	—	—	**6**	—	**7**	**8**	**9**
Mean Impairment Score	0.0–1.5	1.6–3.2	3.3–4.1	4.2	4.4	4.6	4.8	4.9	5.0	5.2	**5.6**	**5.8**	**6.0**	**6.1**	**6.3**	**6.5**	**6.8**	**7.3+**
Percent Domains Impaired	0	1–17	18–24	25	33	35	40	43	46	48	**50**	**60**	**64**	**67**	**75**	**80**	**83**	**84+**
Percentiles:	1–50	51–75	75–84	85	86	87	88	89	90	91	92	93	94	95	96	97	98	99+

(cont.)

BFIS Quick Screen: Self-Report Score Sheet for Raw Scores (All Ages) *(page 2 of 2)*

Raw Score Percentiles (Ages 60–89)

Percentiles:	1–50	51–75	76–84	85	86	87	88	89	90	91	92	93	94	95	96	97	98	99+
Home–family	0	1	2–3	—	—	—	4	—	—	—	—	**5**	—	—	—	**6**	—	**7–9**
Home–chores	0–1	2	3–4	—	—	5	—	—	—	—	—	—	6	—	—	—	**7**	**8–9**
Work	0	1–2	3	—	—	—	—	—	4	—	—	5	—	—	—	**6**	—	**7–9**
Social–friends	0	1	2	—	—	3	—	—	—	4	—	—	5	—	—	**6**	—	**7–9**
Education	0	1	2–3	4	—	—	—	—	—	5	—	—	6	—	—	**7**	**8**	**9**
Self-care routines	0	1	—	—	—	—	2	—	3	4	—	—	—	5	—	**6**	—	**7–9**
Mean Impairment Score	0.0–1.0	1.1–2.2	2.3–3.0	3.1	3.3	3.5	3.6	3.7	4.0	4.2	4.4	4.8	5.0	5.2	5.3	**5.5**	**6.0**	**6.6+**
Percent Domains Impaired	0	1–10	11–15	16	17	18	20	22	24	25	33	37	40	45	**50**	**60**	**75**	**76+**
Percentiles:	1–50	51–75	75–84	85	86	87	88	89	90	91	92	93	94	95	96	97	98	99+

Note. Numbers in **boldface** type in each row (representing a specific domain) indicate the start of the range of impairment for that domain (93rd–95th percentile), compared to the *entire* normative sample. Scores at or above this number are considered "impaired" and contribute to the computation of the Percent Domains Impaired score.

References

Alderman, N., Burgess, P. W., Knight, C., & Henman, C. (2003). Ecological validity of a simplified version of the Multiple Errands Shopping Test. *Journal of the International Neuropsychological Society, 9*, 31–44.

American Educational Research Association, American Psychological Association, & National Council on Measurement in Education. (1999). *Standards for educational and psychological testing* (2nd ed.). Washington, DC: American Educational Research Association.

American Heritage dictionary of the English language (4th ed.). (2000). Boston: Houghton Mifflin.

American Heritage medical dictionary. (2008). Boston: Houghton Mifflin.

American Medical Association. (2008). *American Medical Association guides to the evaluation of permanent impairment* (6th ed.). Chicago: Author.

American Psychiatric Association. (2000). *Diagnostic and statistical manual of mental disorders* (4th ed., text rev.). Washington, DC: Author.

Americans with Disabilities Act of 1990 (P.L. 101-336) and the ADA Amendments Act of 2008. Retrieved from *www.ada.gov*

Barkley, R. A. (1997). *ADHD and the nature of self-control*. New York: Guilford Press.

Barkley, R. A. (2011a). *Barkley Adult ADHD–IV Rating Scale (BAARS-IV)*. New York: Guilford Press.

Barkley, R. A. (2011b). *Barkley Deficits in Executive Functioning Scale (BDEFS)*. New York: Guilford Press.

Barkley, R. A., & Cox, D. J. (2007). A review of driving risks and impairments associated with attention-deficit/hyperactivity disorder and the effects of stimulant medication on driving performance. *Journal of Safety Research, 38*, 113–128.

Barkley, R. A., & Fischer, M. (2011). Predicting impairment in occupational functioning in hyperactive children as adults: Self-reported executive function (EF) deficits vs. EF tests. *Developmental Neuropsychology, 36*(2), 137–161.

Barkley, R. A., Knouse, L. E., & Murphy, K. R. (in press). Correspondence and disparity in the self and other ratings of current and childhood symptoms and impairments in adults with ADHD. *Psychological Assessment*.

Barkley, R. A., & Murphy, K. (1998). *Attention-deficit hyperactivity disorder: A clinical workbook* (2nd ed.). New York: Guilford Press.

Barkley, R. A., & Murphy, K. (2006). *Attention-deficit hyperactivity disorder: A clinical workbook* (3rd ed.). New York: Guilford Press.

Barkley, R. A., & Murphy, K. R. (2010). Impairment in occupational functioning and adult ADHD: The predictive utility of executive function (EF) ratings versus EF tests. *Archives of Clinical Neuropsychology, 25*(3), 157–173.

Barkley, R. A., & Murphy, K. R. (in press). The nature of executive function (EF) deficits in daily life activities in adults with ADHD and their relationship to EF tests. *Journal of Psychopathology and Behavioral Assessment.*

Barkley, R. A., Murphy, K. R., & Fischer, M. (2008). *ADHD in adults: What the science says.* New York: Guilford Press.

Barkley, R. A., Murphy, K. R., O'Connell, T., Anderson, D., & Connor, D. F. (2006). Effects of two doses of alcohol on simulator driving performance in adults with attention deficit hyperactivity disorder. *Neuropsychology, 20,* 77–87.

Bogod, N. M., Mateer, C. A., & MacDonald, S. W. S. (2003). Self-awareness after traumatic brain injury: A comparison of measures and their relationship to executive functions. *Journal of the International Neuropsychological Society, 9,* 450–458.

Bohn, K., Doll, H. A., Cooper, Z., O'Connor, M., Palmer, R. L., & Fairburn, C. G. (2008). The measurement of impairment due to eating disorder psychopathology. *Behaviour Research and Therapy, 46,* 1105–1110.

Booksh, R. L., Pella, R. D., Singh, A. N., & Gouvier, W. D. (2010). Ability of college students to simulate ADHD on objective measures of attention. *Journal of Attention Disorders, 13,* 325–338.

Bryant, F. B. (2000). Assessing the validity of measurement. In L. G. Grim & P. R. Yarnold (Eds.), *Reading and understanding more multivariate statistics* (pp. 99–146). Washington, DC: American Psychological Association.

Burgess, P. W., Alderman, N., Evans, J., Emslie, H., & Wilson, B. A. (1998). The ecological validity of tests of executive function. *Journal of the International Neuropsychological Society, 4,* 547–558.

Chaytor, N., Schmitter-Edgecombe, M., & Burr, R. (2006). Improving the ecological validity of executive functioning assessment. *Archives of Clinical Neuropsychology, 21,* 217–227.

Cook, T. D., & Campbell, D. T. (1979). *Quasi-experimentation: Design and analysis issues for field settings.* Chicago: Rand McNally.

Davies, G. R. (2008). The Psychiatric Impairment Rating Scale: Is it a valid measure? *Australian Psychologist, 43,* 205–212.

Derogatis, L. (1986). *Manual for the Symptom Checklist 90—Revised (SCL-90-R).* Baltimore: Author.

Frazier, T. W., Frazier, A. R., Busch, R. M., Kerwood, M. A., & Demaree, H. A. (2008). Detection of simulated ADHD and reading disorder using symptom validity measures. *Archives of Clinical Neuropsychology, 23,* 501–509.

Friedman, H. S., Tucker, J. S., Schwartz, J. E., Tomlinson-Keasey, C., Martin, L. R., Wingard, D. L., et al. (1995). Psychosocial and behavioral predictors of longevity: The aging and death of the "Termites." *American Psychologist, 50,* 69–78.

Frisch, M. B., Cornell, J., Villaneuva, M., & Retzlaff, P. J. (1992). Clinical validation of the Quality of Life Inventory: A measure of life satisfaction for use in treatment planning and outcome assessment. *Psychological Assessment, 4,* 92–101.

Fuster, J. M. (1997). *The prefrontal cortex* (3rd ed.). Philadelphia: Lippincott-Raven.

Goldstein, S., & Naglieri, J. A. (Eds.). (2009). *Assessing of impairment: From theory to practice.* New York: Springer.

Gordon, M., Antshel, K., Faraone, S., Barkley, R., Lewandowski, L., Hudziak, J., et al. (2006). Symptoms versus impairment: The case for respecting DSM-IV's Criterion D. *Journal of Attention Disorders, 9,* 465–475.

Gordon, M., & Keiser, S. (Eds.). (1998). *Accommodations in higher education under the Americans with Disabilities Act (ADA): A no-nonsense guide for clinicians, educators, administrators, and lawyers.* New York: Guilford Press and GSI Publications.

Harrison, A. G., Edwards, M. J., & Parker, K. C. H. (2007). Identifying students faking ADHD: Preliminary findings and strategies for detection. *Archives of Clinical Neuropsychology, 22,* 577–588.

Hummer, T. A., Kronenberger, W. G., Wang, Y., Dunn, D. W., Mosier, K. M., Kalnin, A. J., et al. (2011). Executive functioning characteristics associated with ADHD comorbidity in adolescents with disruptive behavior disorders. *Journal of Abnormal Child Psychology, 39*(1), 11–19.

Jacobson, N. S., Roberts, L. J., Berns, S. B., & McGlinchey, J. B. (1999). Methods for defining and determining the clinical significance of treatment effects: Description, application, and alternatives. *Journal of Consulting and Clinical Psychology, 67,* 300–307.

Jacobson, N. S., & Truax, P. (1991). Clinical significance: A statistical approach to defining meaningful change in psychotherapy research. *Journal of Consulting and Clinical Psychology, 59,* 12–19.

Jastak, J., & Wilkinson, G. (1993). *Wide Range Achievement Test 3.* Wilmington, DE: Jastak Associates.

Johnson, D. R., & Meile, R. L. (1981). Does dimensionality bias in Langner's 22-Item Index affect the validity of social status comparisons?: An empirical investigation. *Journal of Health and Social Behavior, 22,* 415–433.

Judd, L. L., Akiskal, H. S., Zeller, P. J., Paulus, M., Leon, A. C., Maser, J. D., et al. (2000). Psychosocial disability during the long-term course of unipolar major depressive disorder. *Archives of General Psychiatry, 57,* 375–380.

Langner, T. S. (1962). A twenty-two item screening score for psychiatric symptoms indicating impairment. *Journal of Health and Human Behavior, 3,* 260–276.

Leclair, N., Leclair, S., & Brigham, C. R. (2009). The medical model of impairment. In S. Goldstein & J. A. Naglieri (Eds.), *Assessing impairment: From theory to practice* (pp. 59–75). New York: Springer.

Leon, A. C., Shear, M. K., Portera, L., & Klerman, G. L. (1992). Assessing impairment in patients with panic disorder: The Sheehan Disability Scale. *Social Psychiatry and Psychiatric Epidemiology, 27,* 78–82.

Leon, A. C., Solomon, D. A., Mueller, T. I., Turvey, C. L., Endicott, J., & Keller, M. B. (1999). The Range of Impaired Functioning Tool (LIFE-RIFT): A brief measure of functional impairment. *Psychological Medicine, 29,* 869–878.

Lewandowski, L. J., Lovett, B. J., & Gordon, M. (2009). Measurement of symptom severity and impairment. In S. Goldstein & J. A. Naglieri (Eds.), *Assessing impairment: From theory to practice* (pp. 5–14). New York: Springer.

Locke, H. J., & Wallace, K. M. (1959). Short marital adjustment and prediction tests: Their reliability and validity. *Journal of Marriage and Family Living, 21,* 251–255.

Lovett, B. J., Gordon, M., & Lewandowski, L. J. (2009). Measuring impairment in a legal context: Practical considerations in the evaluation of psychiatric and learning disabilities. In S. Goldstein & J. A. Naglieri (Eds.), *Assessing impairment: From theory to practice* (pp. 93–103). New York: Springer.

Luria, A. R. (1966). *Higher cortical functions in man.* New York: Basic Books.

Merriam-Webster's Medical Dictionary. (2007). Springfield, MA: Merriam-Webster.

Mosby's Medical Dictionary (8th ed.). (2009). St. Louis, MO: Mosby.

Mundt, J. C., Marks, I. M., Swear, M. K., & Griest, J. H. (2002). The Work and Social Adjustment Scale: A simple measure of impairment in functioning. *British Journal of Psychiatry, 180,* 461–464.

Murphy, K. R., & Gordon, M. (2006). Assessment of adults with ADHD. In R. A. Barkley, *Attention-deficit hyperactivity disorder: A handbook for diagnosis and treatment* (3rd ed., pp. 425–451). New York: Guilford Press.

Parker, G., Tully, L., Olley, A., & Barnes, C. (2007). Validity and utility of patients' daily ratings of mood and impairment in clinical trials of bipolar disorder. *Acta Psychiatrica Scandinavica, 115*, 366–371.

Parmegiani, J., Lovell, D., Skinner, Y., & Milton, R. (2001). *Psychiatric Impairment Rating Scale.* Sydney, Australia: Authors.

Patterson, D. A., & Lee, M. S. (1995). Field trial of the Global Assessment of Functioning Scale—Modified. *American Journal of Psychiatry, 152*, 1386–1388.

Pincus, H. A., Kennedy, C., Simmens, S. J., Goldman, H. H., Sirovatka, P., & Sharfstein, S. S. (1991). Determining disability due to mental impairment: APA's evaluation of Social Security Administration guidelines. *American Journal of Psychiatry, 148*, 1037–1043.

Ready, R. E., Stierman, L., & Paulsen, J. S. (2001). Ecological validity of neuropsychological and personality measures of executive functions. *The Clinical Neuropsychologist, 15*, 314–323.

Safren, S. A., Sprich, S. E., Cooper-Vince, C., Knouse, L. E., & Lerner, J. A. (2010). Life impairments in adults with medication-treated ADHD. *Journal of Attention Disorders, 13*, 524–531.

Sheehan, D. V. (1983). *The Sheehan Disability Scale.* Tampa, FL: Author.

Sheehan, D. V., Harnett-Sheehan, K., & Raj, B. A. (1996). The measurement of disability. *International Clinical Psychopharmacology, 11*, 89–95.

Skinner, H. A. (1994). *Computerized Lifestyle Assessment.* North Tonawanda, NY: Multi-Health Systems.

Social Security Administration. (2008). *Disability evaluation under Social Security* (Publication No. 64-039, ICN 468600). Washington, DC: U.S. Department of Health and Human Services.

Sollman, M. J., Ranseen, J. D., & Berry, D. T. R. (2010). Detection of feigned ADHD in college students. *Psychological Assessment, 22*, 325–335.

Stuss, D. T., & Benson, D. F. (1986). *The frontal lobes.* New York: Raven Press.

Suhr, J., Hammers, D., Dobbins-Buckland, K., Zimak, E., & Hughes, C. (2008). The relationship of malingering test failure to self-reported symptoms and neuropsychological findings in adults referred for ADHD evaluation. *Archives of Clinical Neuropsychology, 23*, 521–530.

Sullivan, B. K., May, K., & Galbally, L. (2007). Symptom exaggeration by college adults in attention-deficit hyperactivity disorder and learning disorder assessments. *Applied Neuropsychology, 14*, 189–207.

Wakefield, J. C. (1992). The concept of mental disorder: On the boundary between biological facts and social values. *American Psychologist, 47*, 373–388.

Wakefield, J. C. (1997). Normal inability versus pathological disability: Why Ossorio's definition of mental disorder is not sufficient. *Clinical Psychology: Science and Practice, 4*, 249–258.

Warshaw, M. G., Keller, M. B., & Stout, R. L. (1994). Reliability and validity of the Longitudinal Interval Follow-Up Evaluation for assessing outcomes of anxiety disorders. *Journal of Psychiatric Research, 28*, 531–545.

Welsh, M. C., & Pennington, B. F. (1988). Assessing frontal lobe functioning in children: Views from developmental psychology. *Developmental Neuropsychology, 4*, 199–230.

Wood, R. L. I., & Liossi, C. (2006). The ecological validity of executive function tests in a severely brain injured sample. *Archives of Clinical Neuropsychology, 21*, 429–437.

Index

Page numbers followed by *f* indicate figure; *n*, note; and *t*, table.